EXAM SKILLS FOR LAW STUDENTS

EXAM SKILLS FOR LAW STUDENTS

Second Edition

Harry McVea, LLB, PhD

Senior Lecturer in Law,
University of Bristol

Peter Cumper, LLB, LLM

Senior Lecturer in Law,
University of Leicester

OXFORD
UNIVERSITY PRESS

OXFORD
UNIVERSITY PRESS

Great Clarendon Street, Oxford OX2 6DP

Oxford University Press is a department of the University of Oxford.
It furthers the University's objective of excellence in research, scholarship,
and education by publishing worldwide in

Oxford New York

Auckland   Cape Town Dar es Salaam Hong Kong Karachi
Kuala Lumpur Madrid Melbourne Mexico City Nairobi
New Delhi Shanghai Taipei Toronto
With offices in
Argentina Austria Brazil Chile Czech Republic France Greece
Guatemala Hungary Italy Japan South Korea Poland Portugal
Singapore Switzerland Thailand Turkey Ukraine Vietnam

ISBN 978-0-19-928309-5

Printed and bound in Great Britain by
CPI Antony Rowe, Chippenham and Eastbourne

PREFACE

The aim of this second edition remains much the same as the first: to help law students present their written work to good effect in academic exams and in other coursework assessments. Unlike some other books which cater for a similar readership, we do not aim merely to provide a series of model answers to questions posed. Although some students may find such books helpful, we believe that pedagogically they are of limited value and are apt, in many instances, to leave a student floundering when a new question is raised or an issue which has already been addressed is presented in a slightly modified form. Neither do we cover the more mundane issues relating to examinations such as revision, division of time between questions and so on, since these are problems which students who are taking law exams will already have encountered and should have mastered in their earlier studies. However, because certain aspects of law examinations are different from other exams which most students will have taken, the aim here is to focus on issues of style and method. In particular, we aim to demonstrate how good students can do justice to themselves by adopting the *techniques* employed by successful examinees. Suggestions are made as to ways in which materials can be manipulated and legal arguments marshalled. And methods are identified by which both essay and, more especially, problem questions can be approached. For reasons of space, we have chosen to limit our analysis to the core subjects of criminal law, the law of tort, contract law, and public law. However, the techniques employed in these areas are broadly applicable to other law courses such as land law, trusts, evidence, and so on. Likewise, although we concentrate on unseen timed exams, our suggestions are also relevant to open book exams, take-home papers, and course work assessments. The chapters in Part A of the book—dealing with problem questions—are not self-standing. Instead, the general approach we adopt is set out in Chapter 1 and is subsequently reinforced and, where appropriate, modified in the remaining chapters. The comments of the authors are in square brackets and in a bold font. Edited parts of the answers are indicated by asterisks.

Though the origins of *Exam Skills for Law Students* go back to when we ourselves were law students, more recently we have been faced with a different version of the same problem as law teachers. Often good students fail to reach their full potential on paper, not because they have neglected or are unable to understand the relevant rules and principles of the law, but because of a failure to master exam technique. The need to *teach* students how to answer law questions and to explain why one answer is better than another has prompted us to think about this problem in a more systematic way and, ultimately, to crystallize our thoughts by writing this book. While it is by no means the definitive guide on exam technique, we hope that it will help students produce work which better reflects their true abilities—and which just might make our task of reading and marking exam answers slightly more tolerable!

In producing this second edition, we have taken the opportunity to update and streamline the material in Part A on problem solving, while the material in Part B, which deals with essay writing, has been largely rewritten. We have also taken the opportunity to add summaries at the end of each of the chapters. Not surprisingly, we owe a great debt of gratitude to many colleagues and friends—in particular Lauren Honeyben, Marc Moore, Oliver Quick, and Phil Syrpis—without whose help, and ideas, this project would not have been possible. We would also like to thank Melanie Jackson at OUP for her patience in piloting the project through to its conclusion.

Harry McVea, University of Bristol
Peter Cumper, University of Leicester

November 2005

CONTENTS

INTRODUCTION

How do you succeed in law school? This deceptively simple, perennial question is asked by every generation of law students. On the face of it there would appear to be no easy answer. After all, those who are awarded the highest marks are not always those with the most information. Admittedly, a good memory, staying calm under exam conditions, allocating time, and writing quickly and clearly all have a part to play. Yet the single most important factor in most instances is, in our view, *exam technique*. While for some students exam technique may be intuitive—they do not have to think about it because they just have it—the point is that exam technique *can* be acquired. It can be learned, provided students are prepared to let go of their old habits and take on board new ways of handling the material which they have been set to master. If students could miraculously transform themselves into examiners and thus see their own work as examiners see it, they would undoubtedly perform more successfully in their exams. The changes required in terms of *content* and *style to* earn really high marks would become readily apparent.

From the outset students should be aware that the thesis underpinning this book—that such a thing as exam technique exists and that it can (and should) be acquired—is controversial. There are three basic views on this question:

(a) Exam technique cannot be taught

First, there are those who believe that what we have proposed cannot be done. Adherents to this school argue either (i) that answering legal exam questions is a skill—something which you either have or you don't have—a skill which it is impossible to articulate and therefore to teach; or (ii) that there is no one method—that each tutor expects something different, with the result that the 'right' exam technique depends on the preferences of each individual examiner.

(b) Exam technique should not be taught

Secondly, there are those who believe that university education operates best by encouraging people to think for themselves by fending for themselves. To do otherwise is 'anti-intellectual'. It would drag good students down and pull mediocre students up, thus frustrating one of the basic aims of university education—to let the talented flourish. Good students, so this argument runs, will get to grips with the necessary techniques without specific instruction.

(c) Exam technique should be taught

Lastly there are those—like us—who believe that exam technique can, and should, be taught; that it is part of the process of teaching students 'how to think'. While there is certainly something to be said for the idea that excelling at exams is an innate skill, skills often need to be nurtured and developed; and although different academics do appear to have their own preferences in relation to answering exam questions there is, in fact, a great deal of agreement as to what is quality work and how legal questions should be framed and answered. As far as the argument that exam technique should not be taught, this smacks of 'hiding the ball' from students, and taken to its logical conclusion could apply to all forms of teaching.

The strongest argument against those who advocate that exam technique is capable of being, and should be, taught is that it is tinged with an unwarranted degree of dogmatism—by implying that a certain way is the 'right' way of handling the relevant materials. This appears to put students in intellectual straitjackets, lending credence to the view that teaching exam technique is 'unacademic'. If this were true, such criticism would be valid. However, this argument misrepresents the context of the case for teaching exam skills as we present it: that there are a number of ways of demonstrating good exam technique, in amongst which the approach we emphasize is merely one. In any case, exceptional students are unlikely to be hampered by our prescriptive approach, but will rise above it. Competent students, on the other hand, are likely to benefit. And while we recognize that individuality and creativity should be encouraged amongst *all* students, the reality of the situation is that students have to sit exams. Although these should by no means be viewed as the sole aim of the educational process, it would be disingenuous to ignore exams completely.

The difficulty we face is that to teach what is in effect a subtle skill, we must necessarily simplify and illustrate our points by way of 'crude' examples. Again, let us stress that we have not set out to write a definitive work on answering examination questions. Neither should students assume that the techniques set out are to be slavishly followed or applied in a purely mechanical fashion. They will need to be 'fine-tuned' and it may on occasion be necessary to adapt our suggestions—jettisoning some points and adding others—to accommodate a student's own insights into a subject or, more pragmatically, to accord with individual tutors' preferences. Indeed, if anything your examiner says conflicts with what we have suggested, follow his or her advice—for that course at least. The aim, after all, is to increase your chances of exam success rather than to reduce them.

Exam objectives

Before we proceed to discuss these techniques it is first necessary to consider what law exams are designed to test, i.e. their objectives. No doubt there are many objectives, but for present purposes we can say that exams are designed to test a student's ability to:

1. Identify legal issues.
2. Display knowledge of legal rules and principles.
3. Apply the law to complex fact situations.
4. Distinguish between the relevant and the irrelevant.
5. Analyse and evaluate legal doctrines.
6. Construct coherent, logical, and persuasive arguments.
7. Work under pressure, subject to time constraints.

As a rule, when marking examiners do not explicitly refer to these objectives; neither do they have a definitive list of points which must be covered, let alone a 'model answer'. Yet despite the scope that this gives for an impressionistic and subjective approach to exam marking, there exists a remarkable degree of unanimity amongst examiners when it comes to spotting good answers. Although it is difficult to say exactly why this is so, it may not be too much of an exaggeration to suggest that an examiner is as interested in the *method* or *approach* by which the question has been addressed as he or she is in whether the student has given the 'right answer', insofar as a such a thing exists. Although there should be a direct link between the way in which a course is taught and the way in which it is assessed, sadly this is not always the case. For example, sometimes the lecturer(s) will pay only lip-service to the theoretical aspects of a subject, yet the exam will require a detailed knowledge of theory. Be sensitive to this problem by looking at past exam papers to see how well the examination reflects the material covered in the course.

What examiners are looking for in determining whether students achieve the above objectives can be expressed at different levels of abstraction, many of which are decidedly unhelpful. At the most general level, they are looking for an answer which is written in a 'lawyerly fashion'. At a more concrete level the examiner is essentially testing three things: (1) whether the candidate knows the material (i.e. 'a question of content'); (2) whether the candidate is capable of putting the material within a good, tight framework (i.e. 'a question structure'); and (3) whether the candidate is able to identify the areas upon which to focus (i.e. 'a question of emphasis'—it will be necessary to give greater emphasis to some points and to treat others with a 'light touch' or perhaps ignore them altogether). The candidate who is able to combine 'content', 'structure', and 'emphasis' in a competent and confident fashion will inevitably score high marks. Even more specifically, your answer must be characterized by a thorough, balanced, and logical analysis of the legal issues, supported by authority (case law, statutory and, where appropriate, academic) and written in a clear and concise fashion.

It is, however, fair to say that most law students know all this already. They are probably used to hearing about their need to cultivate the skill of systematic legal analysis—the so-called hallmark of an accomplished lawyer. But for many, either it does not sink in, or they do not know exactly what it means when it comes to answering exam questions. They are unsure of what questions to ask themselves in order to structure their answers; they do not know how to identify the relevant legal issues, analyse them, or introduce and manipulate supporting authority. There is, of course, nothing particularly mysterious about these tasks. All one has to do is to open a law report or a law journal. In the former you will see how judges address legal issues, present arguments, and cite relevant authorities; in the official law reports, such as the appeal cases, just before the start of the judgments, you can see how this is done by counsel for each party. In law journals the process is repeated, either in the longer articles or in the much shorter case-notes and comments. Ultimately, these are the models you should emulate in terms of style and technique and it is from these sources that we draw many of our ideas and some of our examples.

But to leave it at that is simply not sufficient. Despite the fact that what judges, barristers, and academics do—address legal problems, present arguments, manipulate authorities, and so on—is similar to what you must do, your task still differs in significant respects. Your questions come pre-packaged, in 'crime boxes', or 'contract boxes', and so on. Generally, when you answer an exam question, your answer is based on what you can recall, and as you are often subject to time constraints, what you write must be both relevant and concise. The most important difference, however, is that in the law reports judges normally focus on specific ingredients (sub-issues) of the particular crime, tort, or whatever is being discussed, rather than on the general ingredients of the offence, tort, etc. The reason for this is that most of the cases you are asked to read are at the appellate stage and, therefore, the legal questions have already been pared down to their fundamentals. By contrast, in the exam you must demonstrate that you understand *all* the basic elements of the legal issue concerned (a crime, tort, breach of contract, and so on), even though you need to focus on the ones which are particularly relevant to the question set. The basic rule of thumb is that you cannot rely on examiners to infer that you know these things. You should assume that they know very little (general knowledge excepted) about the subject and that it is up to you to provide an appropriate explanation of the relevant issues. The rest of this book is aimed at advising students how this can be done to good effect.

Types of exam questions

The starting point for our discussion of exam technique concerns the nature of the questions with which law students are faced. Basically, these are of two types: problem questions and essay questions. Although in some respects a good essay answer will display all of the hallmarks of a good problem answer (in that it will contain a logical and well-written analysis of the legal issues posed, supported by authority), the approach required for each is essentially different. The student who fails to grasp this important point at the outset of his or her studies will fail to do justice to all the hard work they have done for their end-of-year examinations.

Because of the different techniques required to answer both essay and problem questions, the book is divided into two (unequal) parts: Part A dealing with problem questions and Part B dealing with essay questions. The reason for this imbalance is that many students studying law for the first time will have been previously fed on an 'exam diet' of essays, and thus answering problem questions will be unfamiliar territory to them. It is not surprising, therefore, that a significant number of students display a natural aversion to problem solving, or have difficulty getting to grips with it. Whether this arises as a result of greater familiarity with essay writing, or because of a pragmatic belief that essays offer more of an opportunity to introduce into their answers material which they have learned but which is not directly relevant to the question posed (unlike problems, which require a more definite 'answer') is unclear. But regardless of reasons, it is simply not possible to excel in your law exams (or in legal practice) unless you acquire the art of problem solving. Indeed, with the correct approach, it is easier to score very high marks in a problem question than it is in an essay.

Despite the fact that all problem questions deal with the same basic legal issue—what are the rights/liabilities/obligations/duties of the parties?—in each subject this takes a different form. We have chosen to draw our examples from criminal law, contract law, the law of tort, and public law. For example, in criminal law the central issues are the crimes which the defendant has committed and what, if any, defences are available. In tort the format is similar, but here we are interested in the defendant's civil wrongs and what, if any, are his applicable defences. In contract the issue is who can sue, be sued, on what grounds, and with what consequences. In public law, meanwhile, you may simply be asked to comment on the constitutional propriety of the events in a problem and a range of sanctions (criminal, civil, or even political) may be relevant to your answer. Thus, although all legal problem questions are in essence the same—and many of the techniques explored in one section are capable of being duplicated in another—there are nonetheless good reasons why in Part A each of the chosen subjects should be dealt with separately. In particular, it makes possible the identification and explanation of our basic ideas in Chapter 1 (on Criminal law), and the reinforcement and modification (where necessary) of those ideas in Chapter 2 (law of Tort), Chapter 3 (Contract law), and Chapter 4 (Public law). The division of chapters also makes possible the identification and application of what might be called 'micro' structures relating to specific topics in each subject which will help you in answering exam questions in these areas. The most obvious example of such a micro structure in Tort would be the 'duty, breach, damage' formula used in answering negligence questions. For an exemption clause question, it would be 'incorporation' (is the exclusion clause a term in the contract?), 'construction' (does the clause cover the breach?), and 'legislative factors' (e.g. what is the effect of EC and UK legislation on unfair contract terms?).

In contrast to the organizing framework adopted for problem questions, we propose to deal with essay questions collectively, since we are of the opinion that the techniques for answering essay questions are unlikely to vary at all according to subject matter.

Part A

Problem questions

1 Criminal law

It is important to note that many of the suggestions in this chapter will be of use in answering questions in other areas of law, and are not only applicable to those areas discussed in this book. The relevant patterns will hopefully become clear as we tackle the subjects covered. Another important point to stress is that each chapter assumes a detailed knowledge of the relevant law—in this instance, a detailed knowledge of the applicable crimes, their ingredients (i.e. the *actus reus* and *mens rea* components of the various crimes) and any supporting authority. In addition, it is assumed that the reader is fully acquainted with the appropriate defences and the rules by which they may be invoked, again supported by authority. While there is no substitute for this kind of familiarity with the subject matter, it is also crucial that your knowledge is properly compartmentalized, otherwise you will have no means by which to access it, and thus no way of processing it in the way required of a good student. Knowledge (properly compartmentalized) and technique fit together like hand and glove.

1 Identifying the legal issues

Whatever the subject area, problem questions are complex stories, within which are hidden a number of legal issues that you must identify and proceed to discuss in a practical, yet academic, fashion. This discussion should involve an outline of the relevant legal principles and an application of them to the key facts in such a way as to reach a credible conclusion as to who bears liability, and for what. Your first and most important task is, then, to formulate the problem not, as is so often the case with student answers, by reference to its facts but, rather, in terms of the legal issues—the rights and liabilities—raised by the facts. Thus, instead of writing out the facts, *think* about the facts and *identify legal issues in relation to them*. As mentioned earlier, in criminal law problem questions the issue will always involve an identification of the crime(s) with which the defendant can be charged—murder, manslaughter, s 18, Offences Against the Person Act 1861 (OAPA), and so on—and the defences (if any) available on the charges alleged.

Of course, at first glance the problem may seem really obvious and you may feel that you have identified all of the relevant legal issues—which indeed you may. Alternatively the problem may seem completely impenetrable, in that you may feel unable to identify any or all of the relevant legal issues. However, the issues are there. In fact, in devising the exam question the examiner has started with the legal issues s/he wishes to test and has woven a story around them. For example, the examiner might decide to test s 18, OAPA 1861/duress/participation:

Question

Alan, a journalist with the *Bloomsbury Bee*, has written an article critical of Cedric, a well-known terrorist leader. Alan's colleague, David, accepts an invitation to play golf at Cedric's country club. After 18 holes, Cedric informs David that if, by the end of the day, he does not bring to him the index finger from Alan's right hand, he will kill David's wife and 3-year-old son. David reluctantly agrees and takes the knife which Cedric has given him. Later that day David drives to Alan's home and severely injures him.

Consider the criminal liability of David and Cedric.

How, then, do you make sure that you have identified the legal issues which the examiner has set? Well, one method, which if nothing else will keep you on the right track, is to make a mental list of all the crimes covered on your criminal law course. This list would contain the relevant offences against the person (from murder down to assault). It would also have all of the main property offences: theft, burglary (different types), deception (different types), robbery, making off without payment, etc. You might draw a circle round both groups of offences to illustrate attempts (and other inchoate offences) and participation. Your list would also contain all the defences, noting any peculiarities (e.g. that provocation is only a defence to murder). This list would then act as your template, with which to identify the legal issues posed by the problem question.

Thus, if someone has died in the question you would know that your answer should involve a discussion of either murder or manslaughter (and if the latter a specification of the relevant type(s)). Alternatively, if the harm suffered was minor, you should look to technical assault or battery; if it was serious, s 18, OAPA 1861 or s 20, OAPA 1861, and so on. Once you have classified the harm you can then focus on the defendant's *mens rea* to pinpoint the most appropriate charge. It is absolutely crucial at this stage that you read the question carefully and that you get the facts, the parties, and what was done by whom, sorted out. If you do not your answer will be off target.

Consider the above example involving Alan, David, and Cedric. In attempting to isolate the issues, clearly you need a working knowledge of the various crimes covered on your course—which you should be able to glean either from memory or from the template suggested earlier. Of course, in reality there are many more offences, some of which would be relevant to the facts, but for the purposes of the exam you do not need to know these—for that, knowledge of the crimes covered on the syllabus is sufficient. Since you are told that Alan is severely injured (and by implication not dead) you should be thinking in terms of either a s 20, OAPA 1861, or, most probably, a s 18, OAPA charge against David—because these are generally the only offences you will cover which involve serious injury (GBH) short of death. Although David intentionally, albeit reluctantly, causes Alan to sustain GBH, it is clear that David is acting under compulsion, so the defence of duress should spring to mind—but, if not, check your list of possible alternative defences. Even a basic understanding of these will tell you that duress is the only option. You should also consider Cedric's liability. After all, the crime is at his behest and he supplies David with the knife which has severely injured Alan. As a result, the issue arises, for example, as to whether Cedric is liable for aiding and abetting the main/principal offence.

That, then, is your *thinking process*. But what should you write? The first paragraph of your answer could set out the relevant crimes with which the defendant will be charged and any defences he might have available to him. Weaker students tend not to do this either because they do not know exactly what the issues are, or because they are afraid of committing themselves to issues that are not actually there or which are totally irrelevant. Your first paragraph might be something along the following lines:

Partial answer

The main issue in this problem question is whether David has available to him the defence of duress on a s 18, OAPA 1861 charge (intent to do GBH). The problem also raises the issue of Cedric's liability arising out of his participation in the principal offence and his threats to David.

Here the answer clearly implies that David is likely to face a s 18 charge and that in relation to that charge he may wish to use the defence of duress. The issue of Cedric's liability in the scheme is raised, although the exact nature of the charges is left to be addressed later in the answer.

An alternative—and probably better (certainly safer)—approach would be as follows:

Partial answer

The first issue here is whether David (D) is, prima facie, guilty of a s 18, OAPA 1861 offence (intending GBH) and, if he is, whether he will be able to rely on the defence of duress. . . .
[You could then go on to discuss these points.]

* * * *

The second issue is whether C is liable as an aider and abettor on a s 18, OAPA 1861 charge. . . .
[You could then go on to discuss this.]

* * * *

The third issue is. . . .

The advantage of this approach is that you do not commit yourself too early to the issues raised and you are able to add new charges as and when you think of them, while progressing through your answer.

Since first impressions matter, your opening paragraph is likely to be important. Therefore, you must demonstrate right from the outset that you are in control of the material. In fact very often the examiner will, within the first ten lines or so, build up a presumption—whether consciously or subconsciously—of the class of mark he or she will award to your script. While what is written thereafter may rebut or confirm that presumption, your introduction sets the tone.

Sometimes students start by writing something along the following lines:

In discussing the criminal liability of David and Cedric it is necessary to establish what offences they can be charged with.

There is, of course, nothing 'wrong' with this sort of approach, but what does something like this really add to your answer? Surely it is axiomatic that in a criminal law exam, you need to do this. Why waste time writing something that is obvious? Other students prefer to write a general introduction to a problem question covering the area of law they have been asked to address. Either they (mistakenly) think that such an introduction is necessary; or they use it as a misguided technique to 'feel' their way into the question. For example, in answering the above problem, student's typically write something along the following lines:

> This question deals mainly with the law on duress which has recently been the subject of much judicial concern, the main issue being whether duress should be a defence to murder. In the widely criticized decision in *Howe*, the House of Lords ruled that duress was not available on a murder charge. Their Lordships were of the opinion that the harshness of the ruling could be tempered by Executive discretion on whether or not to prosecute.
>
> Here David will be charged with . . .

Although opinions vary slightly, introductions of the above type are best avoided when answering a problem question. While generally you will not lose marks by adopting the above approach, you are unlikely to gain many either. Why? It is not that what has been written is incorrect, but rather that the student's knowledge has been misdirected. This sort of introduction fails to focus on the question posed: the criminal liability of David and Cedric. Instead, it goes off at a tangent, discussing issues which are not germane to the question. This serves as a reminder that doing well in exams is as much about knowing what to leave out (because it is not strictly relevant) as it is about knowing what to include. As we suggested earlier, one of the purposes of exams is to see whether students can distinguish the relevant from the irrelevant. In answering a problem question you should address yourself directly to the question asked and answer it as concisely as possible.

Sometimes students begin answers by summarizing the facts of the problem. This, too, should really be avoided. The examiner knows the facts: he or she will have set the problem, and if not, will have a copy of it to hand. The facts should be used sparingly, and only in relation to the application of legal principles to them, or when you are attempting to distinguish your fact pattern from a case which prima facie applies to it.

Another commonly used student approach is to begin an answer by stating that the facts of the problem bear a resemblance to the facts of a particular case studied. For example, if the question is:

> D, who was drunk, set fire to an hotel in which a number of people were residing. The fire was discovered before any serious damage was done and none of the hotel guests were injured.
>
> **Discuss.**

A typical student answer might read something like this:

> The facts in the problem are similar to the facts of *R v Caldwell*, where it was held that 'recklessness' for the purposes of criminal damage meant objective recklessness, i.e. not foreseeing an obvious risk that property will be damaged or foreseeing the risk but carrying on regardless . . .

Such an approach is, however, problematic. For a start, the case which the student has cited is no longer good law: *Caldwell* has now been overruled by the House of Lords in *R v G* [2004] 1 AC 1034, and 'recklessness' in this context now bears a 'subjective' meaning.

(As an aside, you may of course wonder why lecturers tell you about cases that are no longer good law. However, students must grasp early on in their studies the difference between: (a) what the law is; (b) areas where it is (or is thought to be) unclear; (c) what the different options are for clarification or law reform; and (d) what commentators think the law ought to be. Your lecturer could have talked about *Caldwell* [1982] AC 341, for example, to illustrate aspects of (c) and (d). Furthermore, some areas of law are better (or can only be) understood in terms of their historical development.)

However, even if the case had still been good law, beginning your answer in such a way would not be considered good style. It is, for example, hardly a stunning insight to identify factual similarities between two situations. By being led by the facts of cases, you are diving into the question too quickly. Instead, your material is probably better presented in terms of the legal issues raised by the question rather than in terms of similar facts. Once you have identified the legal issues (admittedly to do this you need to *think* about cases with similar facts), you can then proceed to set out any relevant law established by those cases and assess whether this case law is directly on point (or distinguishable on its facts).

To recap, there is no need to write a traditional essay-type introduction, neither is there any need to launch into a long-winded regurgitation of the facts of the problem or to start off comparing it to cases with similar facts. Instead your answer needs to cut to the heart of the problem through the identification of pertinent legal issues. As we shall see in the next section, your analysis needs to be pithy and supported by authority at every opportunity.

2 Structuring your answer

In view of time constraints and other exam pressures it is not surprising that most students fail to structure their answers. But although such a failure is understandable, it does not excuse the 'stream of consciousness' approach which many students adopt in exams. Answers typically lurch from one point to the next, and students seem to have no particular objective in mind other than unloading on to the answer booklet as much as possible of what they have learned. Structure is, however, absolutely crucial, and it is false economy—except in a genuine emergency—to launch straight into your answer without taking some time to think about how you will present your material. An examiner wants to read a clear, well-thought-out script in much the same way that a student wants to listen to a clear, well-thought-out lecture. More students would do well to remember that a little information can go a long way if it is presented in a clear, concise, and digestible fashion; and that students who are awarded the highest marks in the exam are not necessarily those with the most information.

Consider the following problem:

> Bernie has an abnormally low IQ. He drives his car to a petrol station and fills it with petrol. He is overcharged by the cashier. Losing his temper, he picks up the cashier's full cup of tea and throws it in his face. The cup accidentally slips from Bernie's hand and cuts the cashier's face.
>
> Bernie storms outside and absent-mindedly throws his still lit cigarette away. It lands in a

puddle of petrol near a car and causes an explosion. Oscar and Lucinda, occupants of the car, are burnt. Oscar dies. Lucinda, after hospital treatment for her burns, is discharged.
Discuss Bernie's criminal liability.

How, then, should this answer be structured? As suggested above, the first thing you must do *in your head* is to identify the legal issues (using, say, the earlier suggested template (see p 4)). In this instance, it means identifying the offences with which Bernie will be charged and any defences that are relevant to these charges. Use these potential charges to structure your answer. In so doing, pay attention to the fact that the question contains two paragraphs, which implies that they are two distinct sets of events which may be handled separately for the purposes of legal analysis and thus for the purposes of structuring your answer. It is perfectly legitimate to split your answer as follows:

- Bernie and the cashier (the set of events in the first paragraph);
- Bernie and Oscar, and Bernie and Lucinda (the set of events contained in the second paragraph).

However, do not overdo this: it is possible to over-organize, or over-compartmentalize, your answer, splitting it into useless sub-headings and sub-sub-headings, which mask interrelationships and which also give it a disjointed, fractured, or 'bitty' appearance.

There follows a very basic plan for the above question, to which we will add more detail in due course. While it is far from perfect, it is nevertheless a sensible means of structuring your thoughts, and using it will help present your material to good effect.

Suggested answer plan

Bernie and the cashier

Under this heading you would write about the offences which you think Bernie has committed against the cashier.

Your *thinking process* might be something like this:

Possibly s 18, OAPA 1861, intention to cause GBH (depending on whether tea is hot, problems with *mens rea*); and, more likely, s 20, OAPA 1861 (maliciously inflicting (a) a wound, or (b) GBH); or s 47, OAPA 1861 (assault occasioning ABH).

Bernie and Oscar

Under this heading you would write about the offences you think Bernie has committed against Oscar.

Your *thinking process* might be something like this:

Murder? No. He doesn't have the necessary *mens rea*; Manslaughter? Yes. Which type?

Bernie and Lucinda

Under this heading you would write about the offences you think Bernie has committed against Lucinda.

Your *thinking process* might be something like this:

Possibly s 20, OAPA 1861 or s 47, OAPA 1861; possibly arson with intent to endanger life or being reckless as to whether life is endangered (s 1(2), Criminal Damage Act 1971: 'aggravated arson').

At this stage you are half way there. You have compartmentalized your answer. All you need to do now is fill in the boxes. How? Having isolated the parties, take each one separately. Then apply what is sometimes referred to as the 'IRAC method':

I   *Issue(s)* (with which crimes may the defendant be charged?).

R   *Rule(s) of law* (here: the ingredients of the crime(s) as constituted by the *actus reus* and *mens rea*). For example, if the offence is murder, state clearly the law on murder, going through the *actus reus* and *mens rea*, all the while supporting what you write with authority (statutes, case law and, where appropriate, academic opinion).

A   *Application of the law to the facts*. Although this aspect is not at all straightforward, it is nevertheless very important, and it can make the difference between an average answer and a very good one. In applying the law to the facts, you must learn to look at both sides of the dispute. For example, in a criminal law question you should use the facts to show how the prosecution will try to demonstrate that the defendant comes within the parameters of the offence(s) as established by the relevant principles. To show that you are aware that there is always another way of looking at the facts, you should also argue how counsel for the defendant would try to demonstrate that the defendant does not fall within the definition of the crime, or, if he or she does, that a valid defence is available.

C   *Conclusion*. Often the problem question with which you will be faced will be set in such a way that the issues are very finely balanced. Do not be put off, however, by the fact that there is no 'right' answer—if there were right answers to all legal disputes, there would be no need to pay for lawyers to give advice. When asked to jump one way or the other, lawyers tend to describe the position they have chosen as the 'better view'. You can do the same. However, do not merely state conclusions; try to make sure that they are supported by reasoned argument. If necessary, outline any difficulties which might lead you to qualify the advice/answer given (e.g. not enough facts).

To summarize: state the issue; suggest the offence with which the defendant will be charged; identify the governing law; apply it to the facts (e.g. stating the arguments for both the prosecution and the defence); and lastly, end with a conclusion.

There are no doubt other structures—or variations on this one (see, pp 69–70)—and if you can think of another good one, use it. For the moment, we will use the first heading to illustrate the processes involved in filling out the answer according to the suggested technique:

Suggested answer

Bernie and the cashier

Bernie (B) could be charged with s 20, OAPA 1861 or s 47, OAPA 1861. Section 20 contains two distinct, but related charges. First, unlawful and malicious wounding; and, secondly, unlawfully and maliciously inflicting GBH. The *mens rea* for both offences is found in the term 'maliciously'. *At the very least*, the defendant must foresee the risk of some harm occurring. However, he need not foresee serious harm resulting, i.e. he need not foresee the wounding or the infliction of GBH. It is enough, for example, that a battery was committed intentionally or recklessly and that serious harm resulted. This was established by the Court of Appeal in *Mowatt* (1967), and was confirmed by the House of Lords in *Savage; Parmenter* (1992).

The *actus reus* of the first charge is a 'wounding'. While it need not be a serious cut, there must be a break in the continuity of the whole skin. An internal rupturing of the blood vessels is not a wound: *JJC (a minor) v Eisenhower* (1983). It has long been established that there cannot be a wounding unless the wound results from an assault. Assault in this context definitely means a battery (see *Beasley* (1981, CA)).

The *actus reus* of the second charge contained within s 20 is 'inflicting GBH'. GBH means 'really serious harm': *DPP v Smith* (1961, HL). 'Really' adds nothing to 'serious harm': *Saunders* (1985, CA). On the issue of whether an assault is a prerequisite for a charge of 'inflicting' GBH, *Ireland* (1998, HL) held that it was not, despite the fact that there the injury was psychiatric rather than physical.

Prima facie, both s 20 charges are sustainable. On the facts, it can be argued that by throwing the full cup of tea in the cashier's face, B foresees the risk of some harm—at least a battery. He need not foresee the harm which actually results. It would seem, therefore, that B has the requisite *mens rea* for a s 20 offence. Furthermore, since the inner and outer layer of the cashier's skin has been pierced, an injury within the meaning of 'wound' has been sustained by the cashier; and given that this resulted from a battery (throwing the liquid at the cashier—so that the requirement in *Beasley* (above) is satisfied) the *actus reus* of 'wounding' would seem to have been established. Alternatively, provided the tea was hot—causing scalding—it could be argued that GBH was inflicted. A conviction on indictment on either count could result in five years' imprisonment.

B might also be liable under s 47, OAPA 1861, assault occasioning actual bodily harm (ABH). ABH was defined by the court in *Miller* (1954, CA) as any hurt or injury calculated to interfere with the health or comfort of the victim. Trifling injuries do not, however, constitute ABH (*Miller; Ireland* (1997, HL)). It would appear that by throwing the cup of tea at the cashier, B did occasion (cause) ABH. The *mens rea* of s 47, which is found in the case law, is intention or recklessness to cause at least a technical assault or battery, i.e. it is not necessary for B to intend or foresee the higher standard of harm, ABH: *Roberts* (1971, CA); confirmed by *Savage; Parmenter* (1992, HL). Intention bears its ordinary meaning throughout the criminal law: *Woollin*, 1997, HL; *Mathews and Alleyne*, 2003, CA. Recklessness here probably means *Cunningham* recklessness or subjective recklessness (I foresee the risk, but carry on regardless): *Savage; Parmenter*. If B did not intend a technical assault or battery (which he probably did), he certainly seems to have been subjectively reckless as to the results of his acts: he foresaw the consequence that some harm, albeit slight, would result from his conduct, but carried on nevertheless. Absent a defence, B is liable on indictment for up to five years' imprisonment.

[* * * *]

Analysis

(a) The IRAC method has been adopted. The first charge alleged is s 20 (I). The *mens rea* and *actus reus* of the crime have been set out (R). Both the *mens rea* and *actus reus* have been applied (A). Lastly, a conclusion has been reached (C). The same approach has been employed with respect to s 47.

(b) Start with the most important *relevant* crime first, then work down. This, however, is only a 'rule of thumb', since if you decide to charge B with s 18, eventually you will hit a dead end. For example:

> ### Bernie and the cashier
>
> Bernie could be charged with s 18, OAPA 1861. The *actus reus* of this offence is 'causing GBH', which means 'really serious harm': *DPP v Smith* (1961, HL). 'Really' adds nothing to 'serious harm': *Saunders* (1985, CA). The *mens rea* of s 18 is intent to cause GBH. Intention in this respect bears its ordinary meaning: *Woollin*, 1997, HL; *Mathews and Alleyne*, 2003, CA. If the tea was merely warm, it is unlikely that GBH would have been sustained. However, if the tea was very hot, then scalding would constitute GBH according to *Smith*. The problem is that even if the tea was boiling hot, Bernie does not appear to intend serious injury to the cashier. **[Normally you are given a hint concerning the defendant's state of mind, e.g. the defendant says something like: 'I thought it was on the cards'.]** Therefore a s 18 charge, if brought, will be unsuccessful.

What you have written is, of course, basically correct, but you have said what Bernie is *not* liable for, rather than what he is liable for. The *emphasis* is all wrong. If you must begin with s 18 here, try the following:

> A charge of s 18, OAPA 1861, for intent to cause GBH, is unlikely to succeed because, even if the tea was scalding hot, Bernie does not appear to have the requisite *mens rea* (i.e. intention) to establish the offence. Bernie could, however, be charged with s 20, OAPA 1861 or s 47, OAPA 1861 **[then discuss these charges]**.

This is a much more promising start to your answer, since it indicates to the examiner that you know exactly why s 18 is irrelevant and what the relevant charges should be. If the question has more issues than you can cover in the time allotted, there is no need to go all the way down to technical assault or battery, unless, that is, you are running out of ideas.

(c) Sometimes it will be appropriate first to set out all the law relating to a charge (i.e. the *mens rea* and the *actus reus*) and then go on and apply it to the facts of the problem (e.g. s 20 above). However, this need not always be the case. Note that in the above answer (see p 10) in particular dealing with s 47), the *actus reus is* set out first and then applied, after which the *mens rea is* set out and then applied. There are no established conventions on which way round it should be done, or whether the *actus reus* should be discussed before *mens rea* or vice versa. In fact, it doesn't really matter (but see p 18) provided the material is set out clearly and concisely, and that it is competently and comprehensively applied to the facts of the problem.

(d) Note how authority is used to support the propositions of law. This is a crucial aspect of what lawyers do—it is their hallmark—and it is fundamental that you employ and perfect this technique if you wish to score well in exams. There are ten authorities cited for the first set of facts alone. Of course, in the answer provided not every proposition which is cited is supported by an authority, but very many of them are. In those instances where you do cite authority it is not necessary to write out the full citation of the cases (e.g. [2006] 1 All ER 123), it is enough to write down the name or part of the name and—if you can remember—the year and court in which the case was decided. Indeed, this could at times be crucial from the point of view of assessing the precedential value of the decision. Underline *all* authority, since this will help to make it stand out in the body of your answer and will create a favourable first impression with the examiner. You do not need to use a ruler or specially coloured pens—a simple hand-drawn line will suffice.

3 Getting the balance right

Although some problem questions may test a student's all round legal knowledge of a subject, often they emphasize certain aspects of an issue (or issues).

A Offences/defences

Since the question about Bernie (above) concerns offences rather than defences (has he any defences?—see later, at pp 29–30), you should concentrate most, if not all, of your efforts on the offences. However, sometimes it is clear that although the defendant may be charged with an offence, he has, in fact, a perfectly credible defence available to him. Adopt a logical approach. That is to say, address liability-creating factors first *then* move on to defensive strategies. Very often the latter are difficult to evaluate in the abstract, and sometimes they are impossible. For example, some defences (e.g. provocation and diminished responsibility) are available only to a charge of murder, so it is not relevant to discuss such defences until you have established that the defendant is to be charged with murder and why.

Question

Alan, Bill, and Charles, who are all drama students, live together in a flat. On the afternoon of 27 June, when the results are released, it becomes clear that all three have failed one particular course option: 'Genre and Significance in Smallville'. They suspect that Dr Death, the course tutor, has marked them unfairly. Alan, who has been in receipt of medication from his doctor to calm his nerves, takes three valium tablets. This is just slightly in excess of the dosage which his doctor has prescribed. Bill, who is already pretty drunk, takes out his hip flask and drains it of its strong alcoholic contents. Charles, meanwhile, is getting more and more agitated and is muttering to himself that he 'hates tomatoes'.

　Bill suggests that they go and see Dr Death in his room 'to sort this thing out once and for all'. Bill opens the door without knocking. Dr Death, who is with a colleague, is startled. He goes towards the three young men and offers them his handshake. Unfortunately, Bill thinks that Dr Death is trying to punch him, so he pushes his tutor against the wall. Alan then takes out his cigarette lighter. Some exam scripts which are sitting on the table grab his attention and he sets them ablaze. He then runs out of the room shouting 'Fire, fire!'. Charles, meanwhile, picks up a letter opener and, unleashing a blood curdling yell of 'I hate tomatoes', stabs Dr Death's colleague in the eye, killing her instantly. Bill is horrified.

Discuss the criminal liability of Alan, Bill, and Charles.

Since the above question is primarily designed to test a student's knowledge of criminal defences rather than offences, your answer should reflect this bias. So, for example, the real issues in the above question are: intoxication/diminished responsibility/insanity/ self-defence. You should be able to work this out from the facts given: intoxication (hip flask—drunk); diminished responsibility/insanity (acting irrationally—'I hate tomatoes'); and self-defence—'Bill thinks that Dr Death is trying to punch him'). Of course, to talk about these defences you must first identify some relevant offences. To do otherwise is, as it were, to put the 'cart before the horse'. But note, for the purposes of this question, these offences are merely the side-issues, since the examiner is really interested in testing your knowledge of certain defences. The point is, you have only a limited amount of time (usually 45 minutes) in the exam to answer the question, so when it comes to making sacrifices, sacrifice the detail on the offences so that you can spend more time on the defences, which justifiably represent the main focus of the question.

Suggested answer

Alan (A) will be charged with s 1(2) and (3), Criminal Damage Act 1971 (aggravated arson) for setting fire to the exam scripts **[briefly discuss this crime, following the rules identified earlier]**. He may seek to rely on the defence of intoxication (through alcohol or drugs). Self-induced (or voluntary) intoxication is available as a 'defence' if the defendant's intoxicated state amounts legally to insanity (*Beard* (1920, HL), *per* Lord Birkenhead). It is also a defence to specific intent crimes (*Beard*), but not to basic intent crimes (*Majewski*, 1977, HL). Since, s 1(2) is a basic intent crime, A could not plead voluntary intoxication. However, in the light of the decision in *Hardie* (1984, CA) A may be afforded a defence where intoxication is self-induced otherwise than by alcohol or dangerous drugs. This is the case here: A becomes intoxicated by way of a non-dangerous drug (valium), i.e. one that is not normally liable to cause unpredictability or aggression. The fact that he takes more than the prescribed dose of the drug does not preclude him from relying on the defence. The crucial issue is whether he was reckless in taking the drug in the first place. It is unclear whether recklessness in this context is subjective or objective, but since the Court of Appeal in *Hardie* derived support from the decision in *Bailey* (1983, CA), it would seem that subjective recklessness is required, i.e. the defendant must have foreseen the risk that the drug would make him unpredictable, aggressive, or incapable of appreciating risks to others, but have taken it nevertheless. Since A takes valium (a soporific drug) prima facie he has a defence available to him. And because he has only taken a dosage 'slightly in excess' of what the doctor has prescribed, it seems likely that a jury would not find him subjectively reckless in taking the pills. If A's plea is successful he will receive a complete acquittal.

Bill (B) could be charged with battery **[a s 47 charge is unlikely given that the recent Crown Prosecution Service, Charging Standards, 1996, require extensive bruising, minor fractures, etc., before such a charge is thought appropriate]**. He will seek to raise the 'defence' of mistaken self-defence. Despite the fact that self-defence is governed by the common law, the question of what amounts to reasonable force is the same as under s 3, Criminal Law Act 1967 (see: *McInnes* (1971, CA)). The first issue to be addressed is whether any defensive action is necessary/justified and, if it is, whether the force used was reasonable. However, the position is different where the defendant mistakenly believes that force is necessary, when in fact it is not. In such a situation the defendant will have a defence if he honestly and genuinely, albeit unreasonably, mistook facts which, if true, would justify him using reasonable force in self-defence (*Williams, (Gladstone)*, 1984, CA; *Martin* (2001)). Applying this to the problem, it could be argued that B does honestly and genuinely, albeit unreasonably, believe that self-defence is necessary and justifies pushing Dr Death against the door. If this version of events were upheld, it would turn what was, prima facie, an unlawful battery into lawful self-defence, and B would secure an acquittal.

However, the rules are more stringent where the mistake is a drunken mistake. There is authority to the effect that a defendant cannot rely on any type of mistake made when drunk (*Fotheringham* (1989, CA); *O'Grady* (1987, CA); *O'Connor* (1991, CA)). It is submitted, however, that this is probably a misreading of these cases. Provided the mistake is of the type which a sober person in those circumstances would have made (i.e. if it is a reasonable mistake) then the defendant would be entitled to a defence. Since we are told that before seeing Dr Death, B was already 'pretty drunk' and that he goes on to drain his hip flask of 'its strong alcoholic contents', it would seem that the principles relating to drunken mistake would apply. But even if the mistake need only be that of the reasonable, sober person, it is unlikely that B would have a defence. It would seem unreasonable for B to mistake Dr Death's handshake for a menacing act which required defensive measures. B is, presumably, in a highly stressed and emotionally charged state following news of his recent exam failure and his drinking will, no doubt, have added to his state of confusion. It would seem, therefore, that B will be liable for the offence of battery. Since battery is a basic intent crime (*Majewski*, 1977, HL), and in view of the principles outlined above, a defence of voluntary intoxication will not be available to him.

Charles (C) will be charged with murder **[discuss this, albeit briefly]**. Counsel for the accused may wish to raise the issue of C's unfitness to plead (which relates to C's state of mind at the time of the trial). However, assuming C is fit to plead, counsel will seek to raise the defences of diminished responsibility and/or insanity (both, relating to C's state of mind at the time of the alleged crime).

The law on diminished responsibility is governed primarily by statute: *s 2, Homicide Act 1957*. It is only a defence to murder (s 2(1)). The defendant alleging diminished responsibility must prove on the balance of probabilities that:

• he has an 'abnormality of mind', meaning a state of mind so far removed from that of ordinary human beings that the reasonable man would term it abnormal (*Byrne* (1960, CA), *per* Parker LCJ);

• that his abnormality of mind arises from causes specified in the legislation (e.g. it is induced by disease or injury); and

• that his abnormality of mind, so caused, substantially impaired his mental responsibility ('substantially' is to be given its ordinary meaning (*Lloyd* (1995, CA)).

It is irrelevant that the defendant knew that what he was doing was wrong and that it was premeditated: *Matheson* (1958, CA). The issue is one for a jury, although psychiatric evidence is admissible to help it reach a decision. A successful plea will result in a manslaughter verdict and sentencing will, therefore, be at the judge's discretion.

It seems likely that C would fall within the first and third limbs of the defence (see above). A reasonable person would probably conclude that C's state of mind *at the time of the crime* (indicated by his speech, actions, and expert testimony) was abnormal. In addition, his abnormality would appear to have 'substantially impaired' his mental faculties—again borne out, most significantly, by the nature of his acts—mistaking a person for a tomato. However, C will find it more difficult to establish that his abnormality of mind arose from the causes specified in the legislation. His best hope would be that it was caused by inherent causes—e.g. that he was abnormally prone to stress, exacerbated by the pressure of exams and the fear of failure. The courts often interpret these causes liberally and are heavily reliant on expert evidence.

Since a successful diminished responsibility defence is nonetheless capable of resulting in life imprisonment, it may be wiser for C to plead not guilty by reason of insanity. The law on insanity is governed by the 1843 *M'Naghten Rules*, which are applicable to all crimes. The issue here involves consideration of the defendant's mental state at the time of the crime. According to the *M'Naghten Rules* it will be for Charles to prove, on the balance of probabilities, that he was labouring under a defect of reason (see *Clarke* (1972)—there must be an inability to reason) arising from a disease of the mind (i.e. an internal factor, see *Bratty* 1963, HL; *Sullivan* 1983, HL; *Burgess* 1991, CA) so as not to know the nature and quality of his acts or that they were wrong. The issue is one for a jury, although psychiatric evidence is admissible to help them.

Notwithstanding the narrow application of these rules, C's plea of insanity could well be accepted. Although the facts are not specific on this point, it is entirely plausible that C is suffering from a defect of reason which arises from a disease of the mind. Moreover, it would appear that by mistaking Dr Death's colleague for a tomato he is unable to comprehend the nature and quality of his acts, thus jumping the last hurdle necessary for the ingredients of the defence to operate. Where insanity is accepted as a defence *to a murder charge*, the judge has no choice but to make a hospital order: *Criminal Procedure (Insanity) Act 1964, s 5, as substituted by the Criminal Procedure (Insanity and Unfitness to Plead) Act 1991, s 3.*

Analysis

(a) Despite its length, the answer is not complete. There are other issues worth mentioning and, if you have time, expanding upon. For example, is Bill liable for burglary—'s 9(1)(b) style'? Has he entered a building as a trespasser and then formed the intention to inflict or attempt to inflict GBH? Since burglary is a specific intent crime to which voluntary intoxication may be a defence, this would have been an interesting issue to raise. In addition, parts of the answer need to be qualified. For example, it is not strictly correct to imply that the burden of proof is always on the accused, since there is an exception: s 6, *Criminal Procedure (Insanity) Act 1964*. Still, your answer does not need to be exhaustive in every detail—tracing the broad outlines of a subject will usually suffice.

(b) Many students are especially weak when it comes to setting out the relevant rules and principles in relation to criminal defences. Often they adopt what will be referred to here as the 'soft-centred approach'. For example, in the above question concerning C's liability, they will rightly discuss diminished responsibility, but the answer will usually go something like this:

Typical student answer

Charles may wish to plead diminished responsibility, which is a state of mind so abnormal that the reasonable man would say so. This was established in *Byrne*. Diminished responsibility is only available on a murder charge. If the defendant succeeds, the judge has a discretion on sentencing, so the defendant might receive life anyway.

What can we say about an answer of this type? The most important point to note is that, despite its rather garbled form, the principles which have been mapped out in it are basically correct. There is even authority, and in the right place too. However, it will not score many marks in the exam. Why? Well, as has been pointed out, it is not enough to cite principles that are correct. To do so is a necessary condition of exam success, but on its own, it is not sufficient. The principles need to be set out within some sort of coherent framework *and* they need to capture the essence of the area you are dealing with; here, the defence of diminished responsibility. The above answer does neither. The most glaring omission (which goes to the essence of the defence, and at the same times provides the framework around which to weave a good answer) is the failure to say that diminished responsibility is governed primarily by statute: s 2(1), Homicide Act 1957. This point is absolutely crucial, because the statute lays down the main rules with respect to the operation of the defence, albeit that they are supplemented by judicial decisions. By using the statute as a 'peg' for your answer, you gain a ready-made framework. You can then set out the relevant rules in a logical order (abnormality of mind, specified causes, substantial impairment, and so on). Indeed, this common failure of students to point out the obvious is part of the wider principle, mentioned earlier, that you must assume that the examiner knows scarcely anything about the subject.

Incidentally, when dealing with defences do not write something like: 'The defendant could raise the defence of self-defence, but it will fail'. In short, you should not raise the issue of a defence unless there is a *credible* chance of it succeeding (i.e. there must at least be a hint in the question that it could realistically apply).

Another good example of the 'soft-centred' approach arises with respect to the defence of provocation where two contrasting partial answers, A and B, are outlined in response to the following question.

Question

Dan has big ears, a fact about which he is exceedingly sensitive. Recently, he has become interested in a classmate called Jenny, who sometimes comes to play with him in his garden. Dan's mother is building an extension to her house, and there are lots of bricks lying around. On a number of occasions, Victor, a boy from next door, has made fun of the size of Dan's ears while Jenny has been visiting. When this happens Dan usually runs away in tears. On one particular day while Jenny is visiting, Victor waves his hands behind his ears and pretends to take off like an aeroplane. Dan grasps the allusion. He walks over to the sand pit, picks up a brick and stoves Victor's head in, killing him instantly.
Discuss.

Partial answer A

Dan can plead provocation, but he must have lost his self-control. But did Dan have 'cooling time' as in *Duffy* (1949)? In addition, a reasonable man must have lost his self-control at such provocation (the objective condition). In *Camplin*, the defendant was 15 years old. He was forcibly buggered by V, who started to laugh and gloat over his sexual triumph. The defendant lost his self-control and beat the man to death with a nearby chapatti pan. It was held that V's conduct amounted to provocation because the defendant had clearly been so angry as to have lost his self-control—and a reasonable boy of that age who had just been buggered might well have responded in a similar way. The reasonable man was to have the power of self-control to be expected of an ordinary person of the sex and age of the defendant, but also sharing such of the defendant's characteristics as was appropriate—a distinction was drawn between those characteristics which affected the gravity of the provocation and those characteristics that merely affected the power of self-control. Since *Smith* (2000, HL) this distinction has fallen out of favour. Lastly, it must be shown that it was reasonable for a person with those characteristics to act in the way he did.

[It is hoped that these principles would then be applied to the facts.]

Partial answer B

Dan (D) will be charged with the murder of Victor (V), which is a common law offence. The prosecution will argue that D threw the brick at V with intent to kill or cause GBH (*Woollin* (1997); *Mathews and Alleyne* (1986)). Arguably, D could raise the partial defence of provocation, which is available on a murder charge only. If D's plea is successful, his sentence will be reduced from murder to manslaughter, and thus the judge will have a discretion over sentencing. If D raises the issue of provocation he only bears the 'evidential burden' of creating a reasonable doubt (i.e. he only has to make the defence of provocation a 'live issue' at his trial). By contrast, the Crown must prove beyond all reasonable doubt that there was not sufficient provocation to mitigate D's guilt to manslaughter.

The law governing provocation is partly statutory (s 3, *Homicide Act 1957*) and partly common law. Provocation is the sudden and temporary loss of self-control, rendering D so subject to passion as to make him, for the moment, not master of his own mind (*Duffy* (1949, CA), *per* Devlin J). Before a successful plea of provocation can be established it must be shown that:

(i) D lost his self-control at the provocation. If there is no evidence that this happened, the issue is withdrawn from the jury. An important question here is whether D had 'cooling time' (*Duffy*: desire for revenge is inconsistent with provocation). However, this must now be assessed in the light of a *dictum* in *Ahluwalia* (1992, CA) that cooling time does not negative provocation—it is an evidentiary matter. It is also possible that the provocation, while slight, would be the 'straw that breaks the camel's back'.

(ii) A reasonable man would have lost his self-control at such provocation. In *Camplin* (1978, HL) the reasonable man was said to have the power of self-control to be expected of an ordinary person of the sex and age of the defendant, but also sharing such of the defendant's characteristics as was appropriate. In effect, a distinction was drawn between those characteristics which affected the gravity of the provocation and those characteristics that merely affected the power of self-control. Although in *Smith* (2001), the House of Lords sought to introduce a more liberal test, this approach has been criticized by the Privy Council in *Holley* (2005).

(iii) A the reasonable man with the D characteristics would have acted in the same way as the D. **[These principles should then be applied to the facts.]**

Which of these partial answers is best, and why? It should be clear that partial Answer A would not get an 'A' (even though it sets out the law on provocation first, before going on—it is hoped—to apply it to the facts), whereas partial Answer B is well on its way to obtaining a good grade. Notably, Answer A fails to place the defence of provocation in context, first, by neglecting to introduce and discuss the issue of murder; and, secondly, failing to point out whether the defence derives from common law or statute law or, indeed, as in this case, from both. However, if there is no murder, then provocation is irrelevant. In developing your material on a particular point you should start off very broadly and then become more focused. You are, in a way, producing a chart for the examiner to follow. He or she must be able to see the overview as well as the detail. Accordingly, the fact that s 3, Homicide Act 1957 is not even mentioned is a very grave omission, and is particularly so given that every law student should know that s 3 plays a fundamental part in the law of provocation. In addition, Answer A is not exactly bristling with authority and, although some correct principles are mentioned, the answer is a bit 'thin' on the law. Furthermore, the case of *Camplin* is handled in a rather pedestrian manner, and there is only a half-hearted attempt to deal with the, admittedly, difficult point concerning how the test in *Camplin* has been affected by the House of Lords' ruling in *Smith*. While difficult points, such as this, do not need to be conclusively resolved, there would, however, need to be greater appreciation of the fact that a genuine problem exists. Lastly, the answer is not up to date, in that it ignores the recent—and highly important—Privy Council decision in *Holley* [2005] 3 All ER 371 (which is intended as a clarification of the present law in relation to provocation, and in which *Smith* (2001) is disapproved).

Of course, Answer B is also far from perfect. For example, if B had 'cooling time' then the defence would fall at the first hurdle, and the other principles that are outlined would lose relevance. You must be careful here. If there is not a lot in a question other than provocation, it might be wiser to present all your material on provocation first and then apply it to the facts. Although setting out and applying the material as you go along is generally considered a more sophisticated approach, how you conclude on a particular point can affect what remains to be said, and thus result in you exiting the question at too earlier a stage. Accordingly, if you do apply the law on cooling time soon after you have raised the issue, you will have very little else of relevance to say. In that case, write something like: 'Assuming, however, that D does not have cooling time, then . . .' and then proceed to write about the remaining material. This may seem a little disingenuous, but it may nevertheless be necessary from time to time. Very much does, however, depend on the particular question set. Equally, *Holley* (2005) is given relatively short shrift, and it would not have been unreasonable to expect more by way of discussion on the impact of this case.

Answer B (and A) should also have considered whether the defence of infancy applied. There are facts which certainly warranted the issue being *raised*, even if it were ultimately to be dismissed. For example, you are told that they (i) were classmates (significant, but not decisive) and (ii) 'played' together. Read every word of the question, all the while assessing its relevance. Facts are there for a purpose and often need to be commented upon.

(c) Handle with care material which is mainly statutory (e.g. provocation and diminished responsibility). Avoid copying out the statute verbatim where you are provided with a statute book in the exam; instead paraphrase your material (see the earlier answer in relation to diminished responsibility). By contrast, where the law on a point derives from the common law, try to be as precise as possible (see, for example, the earlier discussion of insanity). By doing so you will be able to demonstrate your knowledge of the law rather than your ability to copy material from one book to another.

(d) You will note that in most of the above examples the principles relevant to the defence are set out first and then they are applied to the facts of the situation. This is a very safe way in which to marshall your material. For a start, it is very clear when it comes to marking the answer. Also it is a relatively straightforward operation to perform in the heat of the exam. However, it is not the only way in which to handle the material and it is not necessarily the best. Interweaving discussions of the law and fact may, on occasion, produce a more satisfactory answer, and will help vary the style of your approach (for more on this, see the contract section at p 71).

(e) By this stage, it may have struck you that presenting your material as suggested could require an alteration in the way in which you take notes. For example, when you read a case on some aspect of criminal law you must know exactly what crime the defendant was charged with, the ingredients of the crime, the particular question(s) which the judges were seeking to answer, as well as the processes by which they arrived at their answer (i.e. the reasoning employed). It may also be helpful to jot down any problems to which the decision gives rise. Thus, if you were taking notes on *R v G and R* [2003] 3 WLR 1060 you might write something along the following lines:

(1) Facts: The defendants, two boys aged 11 and 12, were charged with arson contrary to s 1(1) and (3) of the Criminal Damage Act 1971, the ingredients of which are: intentionally or recklessly destroying or damaging property belonging to another.

(2) The key question the court had to decide involved: the meaning of the word 'reckless' as used in the section—did it bear a subjective or objective meaning?

(3) Decision: The House of Lords (lead by Lord Bingham) held that the test for recklessness in this context was subjective (i.e. did D foresee the creation of a risk and unjustifiably carry on regardless?). *Caldwell*, which endorsed an objective test (where D could be said to have been reckless even though he gave no thought to the risk he had created), was overruled.

Their Lordships reasoning was as follows:

(1) Conviction for a serious crime requires the D's state of mind to be culpable—here the D's state of mind was not culpable.

(2) The '*Caldwell* test' ran counter to their Lordships' sense of fairness—*Caldwell* was offensive to principle and was apt to cause injustice.

(3) It was neither moral nor just to convict a D, least of all a child, on the strength of what someone else would have apprehended if D himself had no such apprehension.

Problems with the decision:

(1) Although it seems to deal with obvious cases of injustice such as *Elliott v C (a minor)* (1983) 77 Cr App R 103 (where the defendant lacked the capacity to appreciate risks), it does, however, seem to go too far in the other direction. That is to say, it fails to take into account the fact that we might, on occasion, want to hold culpable the thoughtless person (see *Ibbetsen* [2004] CLJ 13).

This perhaps over-simplifies matters, because some cases stand for a number of propositions. Nonetheless, it gives you some idea of what you should be looking out for. Do not transcribe huge passages from the law report to your note-book. Try as best you can to express the ideas you are dealing with in your own words. That way you will be forced to think more about what you are studying and it will probably help you to remember the material. One last point. Cases are not only important in terms of outlining the 'tests'—the appropriate legal standards by which to assess liability/the conferral of rights (see p 29)—they are also a useful source of material with which to criticize the law (read a minority judgment: see, e.g. *Brown* [1994] 1 AC 212, HL (Lords Mustill and Slynn; and *Hinks* [2001] 2 AC 241, HL).

(f) It is common for student answers to contain some facetious remark relating to the facts of the question (e.g. in the above question on Alan, Bill, and Charles, something about 'drama students'). Don't. Such remarks are rarely as funny as you think they are and it makes your answer seem unprofessional.

(g) You may also have noticed the length of the Alan, Bill, and Charles answer. In particular, it may have struck you as unfeasibly long. It is, of course, important that your answer is comprehensive in terms of identifying the main issues while at the same time being as concise as possible in discussing those issues. However, it is unusual for a short answer to score a very high mark. That being said, examiners are well aware of the time constraints you are working under, so your answer does not need to be exhaustive in every detail. Although you do need to give the appropriate slant to your answer, if you do so by ignoring altogether other aspects of the question you will undoubtedly be penalized, even though the material you have covered has been well presented. This is simply another way of saying that you get more marks for covering everything quite well than some things brilliantly and other things not at all or poorly.

B The 'issue within the issue'

Often the key issue within a problem question (generally some particular aspect/ ingredient of an offence or defence) will be hidden behind, or within, other issues. For example, someone may die, and the 'ultimate' issue will be whether the defendant is liable for murder or manslaughter. You will show this by demonstrating that all the ingredients of the particular crime you have chosen are indeed present. However, rather than giving all of these ingredients equal weight, the examiner may expect you to focus on one particular ingredient, even though the others must still be mentioned and commented upon. In other words, the part of the question the examiner really wants you to focus on is not so much to do with the ultimate issue (which must nonetheless be discussed) but is, in fact, more to do with what will be called here the 'issue within the issue'—i.e. some particular ingredient which must be established in order to resolve the ultimate issue. Causation illustrates both the 'issue within the issue' point and another problem to which we shall return later—that of stamping some sort of coherent order, or categorization, on an apparently amorphous set of case law.

Question

Anne and John dislike one another. One day Anne hits John over the head with a plank of wood. John falls to the ground, concussed and in need of hospital treatment. On the way to the hospital, another vehicle, driven by Nicky, collides with the ambulance, which was stationary at traffic lights. On his arrival at the hospital, the stretcher on which John is lying is dropped. He dies a week later. There is evidence that a blood clot sustained from the beating was exacerbated by the crash and the accident on the stretcher.

Discuss Anne's criminal liability.

Clearly the main issue here is whether Anne will be liable for John's death, either on a murder charge, or on a charge of manslaughter (gross negligence or unlawful and dangerous act—you must always specify the type of manslaughter with which the defendant has been charged). Whatever the charge, all of the elements will have to be proved. On the basis of either charge, the *actus reus* (which is basically the same in both instances) will have to be proved (i.e. causing death). In other words, although on the face of it the issue is about Anne's liability for murder or manslaughter, the real issue—the so-called 'issue within the issue'—is whether Anne caused John's death, or whether there is a break in the chain of causation which absolves her of criminal liability for J's death.[1] It should be noted that 'causation' is part of the *actus reus* of an offence (e.g 'result crimes' are comprised of an 'act' in 'legally relevant circumstances' which have 'caused' the prohibited result).

Again, do not jump in. Your material must be set out in some sort of sensible order. Start off with the various charges and then work through the problem. There is a plausible case for murder (Anne appears to intend to cause GBH), so start with the *mens rea* of murder. If the *mens rea* is not clear (and there is no indication in the question that it is), try the *mens rea* of the relevant manslaughter charges. You will definitely find sufficient *mens rea* to establish manslaughter. Given that the *actus reus* for murder and manslaughter is the same, you can take both together (assuming you have demonstrated the *mens rea* of murder).

---

1. Of course, other non-fatal offences against the person would be relevant if causation for murder/ manslaughter were not established.

Suggested answer

[*   *   *   *]

[Having established the *mens rea* of murder (or manslaughter), the crucial question is whether A has caused J's death.]

In order to establish causation, it must be shown that A was not only the factual (or 'but for') cause of the incident, but that she was also the legal cause (i.e. her actions amounted to a 'significant contribution' outside the *de minimus* principle: *Pagett* (1983, CA); *Cheshire* (1991, CA). By contrast, legal causation is based on 'remoteness of consequences' and so the question arises whether there has been an independent intervening act—a *novus actus interveniens*—which will break the chain of causation as in *Jordan* (1956, CA) (on the basis that the doctor's treatment was 'palpably wrong'). However, in *Smith* (1959, CA), *Jordan* was distinguished and was said to be a case on special facts. Accordingly, apart from a completely overwhelming event, the courts have demonstrated a distinct reluctance to hold that an intervening act exists (see: *McKechnie* (1992, CA); and *Empress Car Co v National Rivers Authority* (1996, HL)).

[Apply these principles to the facts.]

Students often expect a 'right answer' to a problem on causation, but more often than not no such thing exists. Instead, simply be sure to discuss the problem sensibly, outlining the law and presenting plausible arguments based on the facts. If this still seems unhelpful, remember to err on the side of caution: very few events will break the chain of causation. It is also worth noting that this answer reduces the relevant law to a set of propositions (i.e. some order has been brought to bear on the authorities).

C Tailor answers to the question asked

It is not uncommon for students to misunderstand or carelessly ignore what exactly it is they are being asked to do by the examiner in the problem posed. At the end of every problem (usually on a separate line) you will be asked to respond to the collection of events which constitute the problem question. In criminal law problems you are generally asked to 'Discuss the criminal liability of the parties', or simply to 'Discuss'. Here you are not expected to act on behalf of one particular side. It may help, for example, to think of yourself as being in the position of a judge. Occasionally, however, you may be asked to advise one of the parties, Ms Smith (in which case you should not advise Ms Jones), or simply to 'Advise the parties' (in which case you should advise Ms Smith, Ms Jones, and anyone else who is involved in the problem scenario). Although it is necessary to consider arguments which go against your client, you are nonetheless obliged to present your client's arguments in the best possible light (but without being biased): good advice always takes account of counter-arguments and overcomes them. Very often students produce a general outline of the law, rather than advising the parties specified.

4   Analysing the rules of law

A Resist the temptation to be led by the cases

We saw earlier how students often begin answers by identifying and writing about cases with similar facts. However, this is not just a tendency in introductions—rather it represents a misguided *method* by which to analyse and present the relevant rules of law. That such a method permeates many student exam answers should come as no surprise, since law courses generally tend to stress the importance of learning cases. It is only natural, therefore, to expect students to write answers that reflect this bias. The following examples show how some pitfalls can be avoided.

> ### Question
>
> Dotty goes to the bowling alley one evening, to get away from her nagging husband. Liz, the repair person, is fixing some machinery at the end of one of the lanes. Dotty, who is in a state of great stress owing to her domestic problems, decides to roll a bowling ball down the alley, just to give Liz a fright. Fortunately, the ball misses Liz, but unfortunately it hits and breaks part of the machinery which Liz was trying to fix.
> Discuss.

As we shall see, suggested Answer A contains certain weaknesses which suggested Answer B manages to avoid.

> ### Suggested answer A
>
> **[Author's note: Possibly attempted ABH; but not attempted assault (assault is a summary offence, and only indictable offences can be 'attempted'); possibly criminal damage contrary to s 1, Criminal Damage Act 1971. The partial answer below focuses on the recklessness aspect in relation to criminal damage.]**
>
> In *Caldwell* it was established that recklessness in the context of criminal damage means objective recklessness. So where the defendant creates an obvious and serious risk and carries on regardless, or gives no thought to the risk that a reasonable person would have, the D will be said at is objective recklessness. In *Elliott v C* it was held that the defendant's characteristics should not be taken into account. In that case C was a schoolgirl of below average intellect. She had been out all night and had had no sleep. Upon entering a garden shed, she found some white spirit and set the shed alight. It was held that she had created an obvious risk, and although it might not have been obvious to her it would have been obvious to the reasonable man; therefore she was reckless. In *Bell*, the defendant suffered from stress psychosis. He used his car to destroy the gates of a Butlins holiday camp and was charged with criminal damage. He argued that because of his stress psychosis he did not appreciate the risk. It was held that although he may not have recognized the obvious risk the reasonably prudent bystander would have. In *Sangha*, it was held that even if the defendant were an expert it would make no difference in assessing whether the risk was obvious. Finally, in *R v G*, the House of Lords overruled *Caldwell* and favoured a subjective approach to recklessness—did the D foresee an unjustifiable risk and carry on regardless?
>
> [*   *   *   *]

Suggested answer B

[*   *   *   *]

For the purposes of criminal damage contrary to Criminal Damage Act 1971, s 1 recklessness now means subjective recklessness—the D must foresee an unjustifiable risk and carry on regardless: *R v G* (2004, HL), overruling the House of Lords' earlier decision in *Caldwell* where an objective test was said to apply. Consequently, unlike in the earlier Court of Appeal decisions of *Elliott v C (a minor)* (young backward girl who lacked sleep); *Bell* (1984) (stress psychosis); *Sangha* (1988) (expert capabilities), the D's characteristics and foresight are now taken into account when assessing culpability. This approach resonates with, but is an extension of, Lord Keith's *dictum* in *Reid* (1992, HL).

[Apply to the facts.]

It should be clear without too much explanation that partial Answer B is better than partial Answer A. Although there is nothing that is 'wrong' with the latter, it is simply too pedestrian. In particular, it reads like a list of cases, many of which are no longer representative of the law, albeit that the answer does recognize this by the introduction of the House of Lords' decision in *R v G and R* (2004). Partial Answer B is, by contrast, clear and concise. It begins with the relevant modern law (which is preferable to an historical trawl through the cases),[2] but is also able to contrast this with the position under *Caldwell* and with the stream of Court of Appeal cases in support of *Caldwell*—such as *Elliott v C* (1983); *Sangha* (1988); and *Bell* (1984)—that have come after it. Moreover, the answer cleverly makes reference to the *dicta* in *Reid* (1992) 95 Cr App R 393, HL, which hinted at a more subjective approach, and which has been more fully articulated by the House of Lords in *R v G and R* (2004).

Lastly, students often talk about a plaintiff or a defendant using X case to support their argument. For example, in talking about recklessness they are prone to write something along the following lines: 'The defendant could use the case of *R v G* to counter the argument that he was reckless. In that case . . .'. Yet again, there is nothing 'wrong' with this mode of expression. However, it is not a particularly sophisticated way of presenting your material. A better approach would be to begin by identifying the legal issue—here, whether D is 'reckless' for the purposes of liability under s 1, Criminal Damage Act 1971. You should then set out the relevant legal rule, or 'test'— which in this instance is derived from case law, the test being 'subjective': *R v G* (you may use the facts of the case to illustrate the rule you have outlined). Following this, you need to apply the law to the facts of the problem question, distinguishing any rules where applicable.

Try to stamp your own structure on the cases (as illustrated by partial Answer B); do not let the cases determine your structure for you (as has occurred in partial Answer A).

B Answer the question on the law as it is, not as it ought to be

In general, problem questions do not require an evaluation of the merits of a particular legal rule or an explanation of the rationale behind any particular rule(s). Rather, they are

---

[2] Though such an approach might be appropriate in a different context, such as a lecture or dissertation.

intended to test your ability to apply legal principles to complex factual situations. A critique of the law is more appropriate in an essay question, which often specifically asks you to criticize the existing law and to suggest reforms. Thus, even if the law you are asked to apply is unjust, or out of date or inappropriate, it is perhaps advisable that you refrain from using problem questions as a platform for change. For example, in a s 20, OAPA 1861 question dealing with a 'wounding', it would not be a high priority—though not wrong—to put forward an argument that, given advances in medical science, the wounding must amount to serious harm (see, Clarkson & Keating, *Text and Materials on Criminal Law* (5th edn, 2003, London, Sweet & Maxwell), 587). Of course, where the law is unclear, or the fact situation is a novel one and is not directly analogous to previous cases, the underlying rationale of a rule may help you to work out whether it extends, or should be extended, to the fact situation in question.

C Impose coherence on confused/confusing areas of law

Certain areas of criminal law provide students with particular difficulties when it comes to exams, because of the apparently 'bitty' nature of the topic. One such area is the law relating to accomplices. Here we will focus on the special rules pertaining to joint unlawful enterprises (if you are somewhat unclear as to the exact relationship between accessorial liability and joint unlawful enterprise you are in good company: see Law Commission, *Assisting and Encouraging Crime* (Consultation Paper No 131) (1993, London, HMSO), paras 1.13, 2.108, and 2.119). The question we want to address in the material set out below, is how these rules—whatever their exact status—might be set out for the purposes of answering an exam question (or part of a question) on the topic of 'joint unlawful enterprise'.

Very often when students approach an area of law, they are confronted with a vast number of decisions which, taken together, resemble islands of single instances, with no coherent principles by which to make sense of them. As a result, the student's task in getting to grips with these decisions appears overwhelming. The danger is that students will allow the material to manipulate them rather than the other way round. The only solution to this problem is to seek to classify the cases, and thus make them more manageable (albeit at the risk of some degree of over-simplifciation). This is an important skill for a lawyer to have, and it is invaluable in the context of exams. The most straightforward means of classification—and it is one to which we will return often—is to outline the general rule and establish exceptions to it. If the material is susceptible to this form of categorization, it will instantly become more manageable from your point of view and more comprehensible from the examiner's (see, e.g. pp 101–102). However, in the answer produced below, a slightly different form of classification is attempted, based on the accomplice's *mens rea*.

Question

Sam and Tim plan an armed robbery on Vera, an elderly, wealthy widow who lives alone. The plan is that Sam will hold her prisoner with a knife at her throat while Tim steals her jewellery. The plan is executed, but after Tim has taken the jewellery Sam deliberately stabs Vera, killing her. Tim confessed that he realized that there was a risk that Sam (known to be unpredictable) might

do that, but he had fervently hoped that it wouldn't happen and would never have gone along had he known that Vera would sustain more than fright and slight injury.
Discuss.

A partial answer is set out below, containing some of the principles relevant to joint unlawful enterprises. Again, the tendency when answering this sort of question is for students to 'jump in' too soon. Instead, divide up the material in the ways suggested in this chapter. For the main part of the question—liability for Vera's death—it might be better to discuss Sam's liability first, and then to move on to Tim's. However, in relation to armed robbery, it would be perfectly acceptable to discuss Tim and Sam's liability together.

Suggested partial answer

* * * *

The following propositions are relevant to Tim's liability for the incidental offence [i.e. **Vera's murder**]:

(a) if an accomplice to an offence has expressly or tacitly agreed to the commission of the incidental offence, the accomplice is also guilty of the incidental offence (*Day* (2002); *Hui-Chi-ming* (1992));

(b) if an accomplice to an offence has contemplated the commission of the incidental offence as a 'real possibility', the accomplice is also guilty of the incidental offence (*Powell, English* (1997, HL));

(c) if an accomplice has thought about the possibility of the incidental offence being committed, but has dismissed it as negligible, he will not have contemplated the offence as a 'real possibility' (*Powell, English* (1997, HL) *per* Lord Hutton);

(d) if the accomplice has not thought about the possibility he will not be liable (*Anderson v Morris*); however, if the offence does not require foresight of the consequences that actually do result (e.g. manslaughter and s 20, OAPA 1861) he will be liable.

[These propositions should then be applied to the facts of the above problem.]

The objection might be raised that many of the above rules are not directly relevant to the question posed—that the answer should select only those that are specifically on point and move on to the next critical issue contained in the question. There is, of course, nothing wrong with such a 'direct' approach, and done properly it will lead to good marks being awarded. However, the advantage of the above method is that it allows you to create a legal template which can be applied to the facts. You are able to demonstrate your legal knowledge and explain why certain rules do not apply and which others probably do. This approach should not be taken to extremes, but it can certainly be used to good effect on some occasions.

In certain instances it may be difficult to work out the boundaries of a rule. If this is the case, it may be helpful to set out a number of different possible formulations of the rule, supported by authority. You could, for example, start first with the most liberal formulation of the rule and work through to the most extreme version (or vice versa).

D The doctrine of precedent and the rules of statutory interpretation

In presenting and applying the law on a particular topic, you must be aware of the importance of the doctrine of precedent. Thus, it is crucial that you appreciate the difference between *ratio* and *obiter*, as well as the possibility of distinguishing otherwise binding precedents, overruling previous decisions, and so on. Failure to do so may lead to the application of a rule which does not necessarily represent an appropriate response to the question posed. An answer which shows no awareness of these important facets of the common law tradition will be penalized. By the same token, if the words of a statute are ambiguous, you must demonstrate that you know how the courts would seek to resolve the ambiguity (see, for example, the House of Lords' decision in *Pepper v Hart* [1992] 3 WLR 1032, specifying when it is permissible to resort to *Hansard* as an aid to statutory interpretation. However, see also, *R v Secretary of State for the Environment, Transport and the Regions, ex p Spath Holme Ltd* [2001] 2 AC 349, HL, where both Lords Nicholls and Cooke dissented as to the appropriate use of *Hansard*).

The difficult issue of working out the *ratio* of a case and knowing which rule to apply in view of the existence of competing rules in different courts, is explored by considering a question on intention in relation to s 18, OAPA 1861. This is followed by a discussion of the issue of statutory interpretation in relation to strict liability offences. There are, of course, many other rules relating to statutory interpretation (and precedent), but since this is not the appropriate place to discuss them, you should consult one of the standard textbooks on legal method.

Intention

Perhaps one of the best (and arguably most difficult) examples in criminal law where the doctrine of precedent has been in issue, relates to the meaning of 'intention'.

Question

Sarah, a first year law student, does not like Dr Nofun, who is the Warden of her Hall of Residence. One night Sarah sets fire to the Warden's flat, causing Dr Nofun to jump from his upstairs window and, as a result, break his legs. When questioned by police as to whether she realized that her actions would have caused serious harm, she shrugs her shoulders and says, 'I suppose it was on the cards.'
Discuss.

Typical student answer

Could the defendant be charged with s 18, OAPA 1861? Yes, I think she could. The *mens rea is* intention. In *Moloney* it was held ... In *Hancock & Shankland* it was held ... In *Nedrick* it was held ... In *Woollin* it was held ...

As we saw earlier, it is generally thought to be bad style to present the cases in this sort of chronological fashion. For a start, the legal significance of the various propositions of law which you cite should be acknowledged. It is helpful, therefore, if you can say whether a particular statement of law is part of the *ratio* of the case or whether it was merely an *obiter dictum*, whether it was said by the House of Lords or the Court of Appeal and so on; and, on occasion, it may be helpful to know who said it (i.e. *per* Lord . . .). It is also helpful if, when outlining the applicable rules, you present them in the form of a synthesis. For example:

Answer

[*   *   *   *]

In general, judges should not seek to define the meaning of intention for juries (*Moloney* (1985, HL)). However, in 'exceptional' cases some guidance might be necessary to help decide when intention can be found (*Woollin*; and *Mathews and Alleyne*). In an attempt to clarify the law, the Court of Appeal in *Nedrick* (1986) said that intention could be *inferred* where the defendant foresaw death or serious *injury* as 'virtually certain'; and that where the defendant foresees the consequences for all practical purposes as 'inevitable', the inference will be 'irresistible'. In the House of Lords decision in *Woollin* (which involved a murder charge), it was said the defendant must at least appreciate that death or serious harm was a 'virtually certain' consequence of their actions. Where this is the case, it would seem that the jury are entitled 'to find' that the defendant has acted with the requisite intention for murder (*per* Lord Steyn).

On the basis that *Woollin* applies to crimes other than murder (which is by no means settled), whether Sarah (S) foresaw the consequences of her actions (i.e. serious injury for the purposes of s 18) as 'virtually certain', is difficult to ascertain. The difficulty arises in determining whether 'I suppose it was on the cards' equates with 'virtually certain'. To the extent that this is established, then following *Woollin*, the jury would be entitled to find that S has the requisite *mens rea* for s 18. However, the expression 'on the cards' would seem to indicate a level of foresight which falls short of 'virtual certainty'.

Strict liability offences

Although by no means the only area where statutory interpretation is important, offences of strict liability pose special problems. You should, for example, be aware that the courts have devised special interpretative rules when determining whether or not a legislative provision amounts to a strict liability offence. These principles were clearly articulated by Lord Scarman in *Gammon (Hong Kong) Ltd v Attorney-General of Hong Kong* [1985] 1 AC 1, PC:

(a) there is a presumption of law that *mens rea is* required before a defendant can be held guilty of a criminal offence;

(b) the presumption is particularly strong where the offence is 'truly criminal' in character;

(c) the presumption applies to statutory offences, and can be displaced only if this is clearly, or by necessary implication, the effect of the statute;

(d) the only situation in which the presumption can be displaced is where the statute is concerned with an issue of social concern (e.g. public safety);

(e) even where a statute is concerned with such an issue, the presumption of *mens rea* stands unless it can also be shown that the creation of strict liability will be effective to promote the objects of the statute by encouraging greater vigilance to prevent the commission of the prohibited act.

In determining whether a statutory provision 'clearly or by necessary implication' rebuts the presumption that *mens rea* is required in respect of some particular element of the offence, the courts will endeavour to discover Parliament's intention by reference to:

(a) the words used in the statute (e.g. words such as 'knowingly', 'intentionally', and 'maliciously' clearly indicate that *mens rea* is required, but difficulties arise where the words used are words such as 'permitting', 'wilfully', or 'cause');

(b) extrinsic factors (e.g. the higher the maximum prison sentence, the less likely it is that the statute will be construed as creating a strict liability offence); and

(c) whether strict liability would promote the object of the provision (e.g. whether making the offence one of strict liability would encourage greater vigilance to prevent the commission of the prohibited act: *Lim Chin Aik v R* [1963] AC 160).

5 Applying the law to the facts

Although we have already touched on the issue of applying the law which you have set out in your answer to the facts of the problem, there are other considerations also worth bearing in mind.

A Mark out the boundaries of liability

It might be helpful for some students to think of the *actus reus* and *mens rea* of a particular crime in the form of a Venn diagram, the boundaries of which are determined by the tests in the relevant cases or statutes. Each new case will alter the boundaries of liability, advancing them in some cases, and sounding the retreat in others. Showing that the defendant's actions fall within the *actus reus* is necessary, but not sufficient (except, for example, in cases of absolute liability) for the offence to be established. Similarly, demonstrating that the defendant's mental state falls within the *mens rea* is again necessary, but not sufficient. When the defendant falls within both sets, criminal liability ensues—the ingredients of the crime are established. For example, the *mens rea* of murder is an intention to kill or to cause GBH and the *actus reus* is the causing of death or GBH. The defendant must, therefore, intend to cause death and, in fact, do so; or he must intend to cause GBH, and do so, with the result that death flows from it. The rules and principles which define the *mens rea* and *actus reus* of murder mark out the limits of liability—they represent the appropriate legal standard for liability to ensue. You must use the facts to determine whether, once these limits have been drawn, the defendant falls inside (using facts which support the prosecution's argument) or, outside (using facts which support defence counsel's argument); or if he does fall inside, whether he has a defence. In other words, in applying the law to the facts you are assessing whether the appropriate legal standards have been met. A well-devised question will give you scope to present the arguments for and against liability, although often the facts tend to point in one direction.

Consider the earlier question about Bernie (see pp 7–8). You may recall he was charged with ss 20 and 47, OAPA 1861. There are plenty of facts that would seem to place him within the 'boundaries of liability' established by ss 20 or 47; but you may also have wondered whether he has a defence. Certainly most laypeople would say that he does— after all, he has an 'abnormally low IQ'. However, this is really a red herring in terms of establishing criminal liability. Why? First, Bernie drives a car, and, secondly, he is capable of realizing that he has been short-changed. Therefore, he cannot be *that* mentally subnormal. These factors militate against him successfully raising a defence of, for example, insanity. You would need to use these facts to indicate why his mentally subnormal state is irrelevant for the purposes of his criminal liability.

B Do not invent facts

Sometimes an examiner deliberately (or perhaps inadvertently) leaves out a fact which you would need to know to express a view on the defendant's criminal (or tortious or contractual etc.) liability. If this is the case, note it and state its relevance. For example, in the question about Bernie and the cashier, the examiner does not inform us whether the tea is boiling hot, warm, or cold. It seems sensible to comment on this, but you should not make too much of it. Indeed, try to avoid blaming the examiner for failing to clarify all the facts of the problem, for although the problem may have been badly set, it is best to adopt a diplomatic approach. Try saying something like 'on the facts of the question there is nothing to indicate that . . .' or 'on the facts, it is not clear whether . . .'. In this way, you avoid impugning the examiner's competence; and it is, on the whole a more sensible strategy, since examiners often mean to leave certain facts vague to allow you more scope for argument. Do not, however, take this leeway as a licence to invent facts at will. For example, avoid saying, 'If Bill had done . . . then he would be liable for . . .'. Likewise, avoid any attempt to make up your own question: 'What if Bill had killed Dr Death? . . .'.

There may, of course, be instances when it is appropriate to make certain assumptions in your answer. But this is a far cry from inventing facts. For example, in the question about Alan, Bill, and Charles (see pp 12–13), since you are not told what sort of harm Bill has caused Dr Death, you should tell the examiner that you are assuming that a particular type of harm has been sustained—thus leading to the charge of a relevant offence—and get on with explaining the defences which Bill has a credible chance of pursuing. In the suggested answer provided earlier, it has been assumed that a minor type of harm has been sustained, thus giving rise to liability for a battery unless a defence can be established. One last point: do not worry about issues of proof, take the facts as given.

C The same rules apply to statutory offences

Usually students experience great difficulty in answering problem questions involving statutory offences, especially property offences. The applicable techniques are, however, exactly the same: the crimes will be limited to those covered in the syllabus (usually seven or eight offences, the most important of which are theft, obtaining property by deception, and burglary). You will need to know the *mens rea* and *actus reus* elements of these offences, many of which overlap. So if the charge is theft, go through appropriation, property, belonging to another, and so on. Remember, however, that there will usually also be an 'issue within the issue' to deal with and, consequently, you will need to give appropriate weight to this particular aspect in your discussion. The question below, for example, concerns whether Billy is liable for theft (but note also, following the House of Lords' decisions in *Gomez* [1993] AC 442 and *Hinks* [2001] 2 AC 241, the applicability of the offence of s 15, Theft Act 1968, obtaining property by deception). In addressing the 'issue within the issue' point (with the emphasis on appropriation), the answer sets out the relevant legal rules in a comprehensive and comprehensible fashion.

Question

Billy hears that people in the next street are moving house and are using the Sunshine Removal Company. He arrives early one morning in his own furniture removal van, pretending to be the Sunshine Removal Company, and starts loading furniture into his van (under the general supervision of the owner of the house). He then makes off with the furniture, only to be apprehended later that day by the police.

Discuss.

Suggested answer

Billy could be charged with theft, which is the appropriation of property belonging to another with the intention of permanently depriving the other of it (*s 1(1), Theft Act 1968*). The *actus reus* of the offence is the appropriation of property belonging to another. Appropriation is defined in s 3(1) as 'any assumption of the rights of an owner'. The question arises here whether an appropriation can take place with the owner's consent (or apparent consent). In *Lawrence* (1972) the House of Lords said that consent was irrelevant for the purposes of s 3(1) (*per* Viscount Dilhome). In that case there was said to be an appropriation notwithstanding the fact that V allowed the taxi driver to take money from his wallet. However, according to the later decision of the House of Lords in *Morris* (1984), there could not be an appropriation if the owner consented (see also *Skipp* (1974, CA) and *Fritschy* (1985, CA)). Today, however, the matter has been settled by the House of Lords in *Gomez*, where it was held that there could be an appropriation notwithstanding the owner's consent. Although in *Gomez*, V's 'consent' had been the result of D's false misrepresentation, according to the majority in *Hinks* (2001, HL) consent need not have been secured in this manner for an appropriate to have occurred (*per* Lord Steyn).

[Apply to the facts.]

If a sensible argument can be made that all the ingredients of theft can be established, then it would probably be a good idea to apply the above rules on appropriation to the facts *before* proceeding to discuss the next ingredient. That way you keep bringing your material back to the question. However, if the question is somewhat 'light' on issues in general, you could find yourself 'exiting' from the question (i.e. closing off your answer) long before you get the opportunity to demonstrate the full breadth of your legal knowledge. For example, if appropriation could not sensibly be established and this were the first ingredient you discussed, you would have difficulty developing your answer on theft much further. Note that having identified the ingredient you wish to discuss, you are required to set out the relevant statutory provision first (though there is no need to write it out verbatim), and then to flesh it out with the various holdings in the cases. Thus, in relation to 'appropriation', s 3 is discussed and then further discussion/clarification is drawn from the cases of *Lawrence*, *Morris*, *Gomez*, and *Hinks*).

6 Writing style

In presenting your material, your style of writing is important. Some students write particularly well. Their sentences flow smoothly, following on clearly one from another. Provided they have the right problem-solving technique, these answers are generally a pleasure to read. Other students, however, write poorly. Either their sentences are too long, with too many clauses, or their material does not seem logical. Remember, you are putting together an answer for someone else to read and understand. It is not the examiner's job to work out what exactly it is you are trying to say. Rather, it is your job to make clear what it is you are trying to say. If you have particular difficulties writing good prose, keep your sentences relatively short. Make sure that your ideas follow on logically from one another; and, perhaps most importantly of all, take complex ideas and try to simplify them.

7 Summary

- Read the problem question very carefully, all the while assessing its relevance. Facts are there for a purpose and often need to be commented upon. Do some thinking *before* you start to write your answer.
- In thinking about, as well as writing and structuring your answer, you can profit by using the IRAC method, where: I = Issue(s); R = Rules of law; A = Application of the law to the facts; and C = Conclusion.
  - Identify the legal issue(s)—i.e. for a criminal law problem question, this involves identifying all the relevant crimes committed by the parties (and any defences they may plausibly have available to them);
  - In relation to the crimes/defences, set out the relevant law and support it with authority (case law and statute as appropriate);
  - Apply the law to the facts, noting any significant factual matters that might render the law cited inapplicable or distinguishable;
  - Conclude as to where liability is likely to lie.
- Essay-style introductions are best avoided when answering a problem question. Instead, you should address yourself to the legal issues raised by the question (i.e. the rights and liabilities of the parties) and answer them as concisely as possible. Doing well in exams is, therefore, as much about knowing what to leave out (because it is not strictly relevant) as it is about knowing what to include.
- You do not need to begin your answer by summarizing the facts of the problem. The examiner knows the facts: he or she will have set the problem, and if not, will have a copy of it to hand. The facts should be used sparingly, e.g. in relation to the application of legal principles to them, or when you are attempting to distinguish your fact pattern from a case which prima facie applies to it.
- Equally, avoid beginning your answer by stating that the facts of the problem bear a resemblance to the facts of a particular case you have studied. Instead, present

your material in terms of the legal issues raised by the question, and use the case law to illustrate any potential liabilities that you have identified.

- By all means use headings to help structure your answer. However, do not overdo this; it is possible to over-organize, or over-compartmentalize, your answer, splitting it into useless sub-headings and sub-sub-headings, which mask interrelationships and which give it a disjointed, fractured, or 'bitty' appearance.

- As a 'rule of thumb', start with the most important *relevant* crime first, then work down. However, avoid going down *long* cul-de-sacs, where you end up saying that D will *not* be liable because some crucial ingredient of the crime is missing.

- There is no established convention on whether you should set out the *actus reus* first or the *mens rea* first or whether you should set out both the *actus reus* and the *mens rea* before you move on to apply the law to the facts of the problem. Although it very much depends on the particular question, it is probably best to apply the law as you go along—bearing in mind, that you may not want to 'exit' the question too soon.

- You must cite as much relevant authority as possible. It is not necessary to write out the full citation of the case, it is enough to write down the name or part of the name, and—if you can remember—the year and court in which the case was decided.

- Adopt a logical approach. Address liability-creating factors first *then* move on to defensive strategies. Indeed some defences are only applicable once a specific offence has been committed (e.g. provocation is only relevant if the D is to be charged with murder).

- Since no answer is ever perfect, you do not need to worry about being exhaustive in every detail. But you do have to reach a point where you have presented a 'critical mass' of relevant material in relation to the key issues.

- Handle statutory material with care. Avoid copying out the statute verbatim where you are provided with a statute book in the exam; instead paraphrase your material.

- Remember that the part of the question the examiner really wants you to focus on is not so much to do with the ultimate issue (which must nonetheless be discussed) but is more to do with the 'issue within the issue'—that is, some particular ingredient which must be established in order to resolve the ultimate issue.

- In general, problem questions do not require an evaluation of the merits of a particular legal rule or an explanation of the rationale behind any particular rule(s). Rather, they are intended to test your ability to apply legal principles to complex factual situations.

- Sometimes an examiner deliberately (or perhaps inadvertently) leaves out a fact which you would need to know to express a view on the defendant's liability. If this is the case, note it and state its relevance. However, avoid blaming the examiner for failing to clarify all the facts of the problem.

- Do not invent facts, or worry about issues of proof.

- Adopt a simple, uncluttered writing style. If in doubt, keep your sentences relatively short and to the point.

2 The law of tort

The purpose of this chapter is to extend the problem-solving approach used in Chapter 1 to tort problems. Rather than simply repeating the advice which has been offered in the previous chapter, the aim here is to select examples from tort law which reinforce the earlier-mentioned techniques. Naturally, where differences or qualifications are required they are outlined. This chapter is, at times, also illustrative of more specialized 'micro' structures around which answers can be arranged.

In terms of technique, the link between the law of tort and criminal law is particularly strong: '[j]ust as the criminal law consists of a body of rules establishing specific offences, so, the law of torts consists of a body of rules establishing specific injuries. Neither in one case nor the other is there a general principle of liability.'[1] Thus, self-standing, or nominate, torts have their own specific ingredients (albeit that some of these are unclear and evolving) in much the same way that different crimes have their own *actus reus* and *mens rea* ingredients. And these torts have applicable defences just as crimes have applicable defences. A quick glance at the questions posed below will reveal that the same basic patterns found in Chapter 1 are played out repeatedly, save for the fact that on this occasion we are interested not in the defendant's crimes but in the torts that have been committed—and against whom—as well as the defences, if any, that are available to the tortfeasor. As with criminal law, you will need a template of some sort—either written down, or clearly thought out in your mind—categorizing the different torts (e.g. negligence, *Rylands v Fletcher*, nuisance, defamation, assault, battery, false imprisonment, and so on) and noting the various legal principles relevant to each. Again, it is assumed that you know these elements and can recall them easily.

Make sure you have distinguished clearly in your mind the difference between these types of torts and issues such as vicarious liability. The latter form of liability does not, of course, represent a distinct tort. Instead it is a means by which some person can be held liable for the torts committed by another. It is, in other words, a means of displacing liability from one person to another (e.g. from the employee to the employer). Naturally your template should also include any applicable defences available to the tortfeasor.

The questions discussed in this chapter focus on liability in negligence, liability under the Occupiers' Liability Acts 1957 and 1984 and the Animals Act 1971, and liability in *Rylands v Fletcher* as well as in nuisance. (Incidentally, given that some crimes are torts—e.g. battery is a crime and also a tort—it is important *for exam purposes* to keep these two bodies of law separate and to remember that different rules apply, most obviously, in relation to the standard of proof, but also in many other significant respects.)

A word of warning about negligence is appropriate. Negligence is a self-standing tort—the tort of negligence—but it may also be relevant to the way in which other torts are

---

1. Quoted in *Salmond & Heuston on the Law of Torts* (20th edn, 1992, London, Sweet & Maxwell) at 18.

committed (e.g. nuisance) and, as we shall see in the next chapter, it is also a way in which certain contracts can be breached. It is important to see the role of negligence in different contexts and to appreciate the variations in, as well as the overlapping nature of, the rules which apply.

1 Tackling a problem question on the tort of negligence

To sue someone successfully for the tort of negligence, the claimant must show *on the balance of probabilities* that:

(a) the defendant *owed* the claimant a legal duty;

(b) the defendant *breached* that legal duty;

(c) the breach *caused* the claimant damage;

(d) the *damage* was not too remote.

(a) = DUTY; (b) = BREACH; and (c) and (d) = DAMAGE

If the claimant is able to show the above, then the defendant may wish to raise a defence (e.g. *volenti non fit injuria* (consent), or contributory negligence). It is probably worth mentioning that most defences relate to the claimant's conduct whereas liability (prima facie) depends on the defendant's conduct.

The above 'duty/breach/damage' formula offers a 'micro structure' around which a negligence answer can be presented. Whatever way your answer is structured—by issues, by parties, chronologically—these areas would need to be addressed in some sort of logical format. This should become clear from the answer to the following question:

Question

Alice, an elderly lady with poor eyesight, goes shopping one day in her local supermarket, Safeco. As she enters the store she is thinking about what to buy for her evening meal. Just inside the entrance there is a display of jam arranged in a pyramid. As Alice walks into the store she bumps into the pyramid, causing it to collapse. Many of the jam jars are smashed and broken glass ends up everywhere. Flustered, but unhurt, Alice continues with her shopping. Safeco lose jam valued at £400. Dirk, who is at the other end of the store, is choosing a frozen turkey at the time of the accident. He thinks that the noise is a bomb explosion and suffers severe shock. Dirk refuses to shop in Safeco since the accident, as the memories are too traumatic for him.

Bill, a 16-year-old petty criminal, has recently been sentenced to do 100 hours community service in Safeco, but receives a small amount of pocket money and his meals while on duty. While collecting abandoned shopping trolleys, Bill begins to fool around. Suddenly he loses control and pushes the line of trolleys into Alice's path. Alice suffers from a fragile bone condition and as a result of the accident sustains multiple fractures.

Discuss.

Before looking at the suggested answer, it might be helpful to consider for a moment a possible framework which you could use in tackling the above question. The organizing framework is based on the various parties (i.e. who will sue whom?) in the question. Once these are identified, the next stage is to isolate the relevant legal issue (here, whether the defendant has been negligent) and then employ the so-called IRAC method (I = Issue; R = Rule(s) of Law; A = Application; and C = Conclusion) set out in Chapter 1:

> Safeco v Alice (negligence?)
>
> Dirk v Alice (negligence?)
>
> Alice v Bill/Safeco?/Home Office? (negligence?)

Within each coupling you can then go on to apply the duty, breach, damage formula, as follows:

Suggested answer

Safeco v Alice

The first issue is whether Safeco (S) can successfully sue Alice (A) in negligence for the losses they sustain as a result of A bumping into the pyramid of jam jars. To do so, S must show *on the balance of probabilities* that:

(a) A owed S a legal duty of care;

(b) A breached that legal duty;

(c) the breach caused S damage ('but for' causation); and

(d) the damage claimed was not too remote.

In *Donoghue v Stevenson* (1932, HL), Lord Atkin laid down two principles which determine the existence of a duty of care: foreseeability and proximity. The test of foreseeability is an objective one and is based on whether a reasonable person in the defendant's position would have foreseen that his actions would adversely affect others. Proximity refers to whether the defendant would have expected his actions to affect a particular person or class of persons. More recent cases, such as *Caparo v Dickman* (1990, HL), have added an additional limb to this test: the imposition of the duty must be 'fair, just and reasonable' (confirmed by the House of Lords in *Marc Rich v Bishop Rock Marine* (1995)). Applying these principles to the problem it would appear that A owes S a duty of care. A reasonable person in A's shoes should have been able to foresee that by acting carelessly she might adversely affect others. There is also sufficient proximity, since it is reasonable to foresee that S would be amongst that class of persons affected. Finally, the imposition of the duty would seem to be 'fair, just, and reasonable' in the circumstances.

    In addition to the existence of a legal duty of care, it must also be shown that A breached her duty of care to S. A must exercise the care of an ordinary person (*Roberts v Ramsbottom* (1980)). Ordinarily, the test is objective (*Nettleship v Weston* (1971, CA)). Omitting to do something that a reasonable person would do, or doing what a reasonable person would not do, amounts to a breach of care. On the facts, A would appear to have breached her duty of care since by thinking of what she would have for her evening meal instead of concentrating on where she was going, she fails to live up to the standards expected of a reasonable person. It is no defence for A to allege that she is shortsighted: *Nettleship v Weston*, where the actions of a learner driver were held to be measured against the standards of an experienced driver. However, it was emphasized by the Court of Appeal in that case that the 'higher' standard was justifiable because the defendant was compulsorily insured. The courts may, therefore, be more generous in their interpretation of reasonableness in the case of an uninsured defendant, such as A.

Next, we must consider whether A's breach was the factual cause of the damage sustained by S (the 'but for' test: *Wilsher v Essex* (1987, HL); *Fairchild v Glenhaven Funeral Services Ltd* (2000, HL)). This would not be difficult to show on the facts. S must also show that A's negligence was the legal cause, i.e. this concerns the issue of whether the damage sustained by S was too remote. In *The Wagon Mound* (1966, PC) it was held that damages could only be recovered for the type of harm that was reasonably foreseeable, albeit that the precise series of events that produced the harm was not foreseen (*Hughes v Lord Advocate* (1963, HL)); neither does the extent of the damage need to be foreseen (*Hughes*). In other words, a tortfeasor is liable to an unlimited extent for all losses caused by his act which are reasonably foreseeable. The breaking of the jam jars would have been a foreseeable consequence of A's actions. However, S would only be permitted to claim for consequential loss, and not for any pure economic loss (*Spartan Steel v Martin* (1972, CA)). Thus, S could claim recovery of the £400 worth of jam and for the cost of cleaning it up. However, S could not claim for the profits lost as a result of turning away customers while cleaning up, or for the profits lost because Dirk does not shop there anymore.

It would seem, therefore, that S has a fairly solid case against A. The latter's only defence might be to claim that S was contributorily negligent, resulting in a reduced award of damages (Law Reform (Contributory Negligence) Act 1945). An example from the case law is *Capps v Miller* (1989) where a motorcyclist had his damages reduced by 10 per cent for not wearing his helmet. On the facts of the question, there is a good argument that S is to some degree responsible for its own misfortunes by virtue of the fact that it stacks, in the form of a pyramid, easily breakable jars near the entrance to the supermarket.

Dirk v Alice

The tort of negligence allows claims to be made for mental as well as physical or pecuniary harms (*McLoughlin v O'Brian* (1983, HL); *Alcock* (1992, HL)). Accordingly, Dirk (D) may wish to sue A for the nervous shock he sustains as a result of the breaking of the jam jars. It is a requirement that the shock induces some form of psychiatric illness. Broadly, the same 'hurdles' are discussed in the above section of the answer apply (i.e. duty, breach, damage). Traditionally the courts have construed the duty of care narrowly in the context of nervous shock. According to *White v Chief Constable of South Yorkshire* (1998, HL), a person who negligently exposes another to a risk of injury can be held liable for any psychological damage this may cause irrespective of whether the threatened physical injury fails to occur (see also *Dulieu v White* (1901), and *Page v Smith* (1995)). The claimant's fear of injury must, however, be reasonable given the nature of the risk and the claimant's position: *McFarlane v Wilkinson* (1997, CA). It is unlikely, therefore, that D will be able to bring a successful claim. D is, after all, very far away at the time of the incident in question ('at the other end of the store'), and it would seem unreasonable, in view of the nature of the risk created, for A to owe D a duty of care. Moreover, D merely suffers 'traumatic memories' which may not be sufficient to constitute a recognized psychiatric illness. (Compare *Walters v North Glamorgan NHS Trust* (2002), where a woman who watched her child die over a 36-hour period was entitled to damages for nervous shock).'

Alice v Bill/Safeco/Home Office

A may sue B in negligence for the injuries she sustains as a result of her collision with the shopping trolley. Again the principles set out in *Safeco v Alice* (above) are relevant. It would seem clear that B owes A a duty of care and that the duty has been breached. Equally, it seems clear that 'but for' the breach A would not have sustained her injuries. The crucial issue here, however, seems to be whether the extent of her injuries was foreseeable, in that A suffers from a fragile bone condition of which B was unaware. Although in *The Wagon Mound* it was held that only reasonably foreseeable damage could be compensated, it was enough to foresee the occurrence of a particular *type* of harm; it was not necessary to foresee the *extent* of that harm. It could be argued that B should have foreseen the type of harm that could be sustained (broken bones) from his conduct. In any case (i) it is reasonably foreseeable that an old lady would have a fragile bone condition; and (ii) B must take the victim as he finds her: *Smith v Leech Brain* (1961). On the latter basis, A's fragile bone condition would be irrelevant for the purposes of imposing liability on B; it would not break the chain of causation.

If Bill has no money or no insurance, A may wish to sue S, who may be vicariously liable in negligence for B's actions. To do this, A needs to establish that B was S's employee (which seems unlikely on the facts). The parties' own labelling of the relationship is not conclusive (*Ferguson v Dawson* (1975, CA)). No single fact is decisive. Factors taken into account include the degree of control exercised by the employer, the degree to which B is part of S's organization, the nature of payment, and the nature of the employment contract (*Ready Mixed Concrete* (1968)).

* * * *

A might also consider suing the Home Office (or the relevant governmental body) for B's tort. The courts have been reluctant to attribute liability for the acts of third parties (*Smith v Littlewoods* (1987, HL); and *Topp v London Country Bus* (1993, CA)). However, in exceptional circumstances (e.g. where the defendant has control over the third party who causes the harm and the third party's actions are reasonably foreseeable (*Dorset Yacht* 1970, HL)), a duty may be owed. Such a duty is, however, unlikely to arise on the facts of this problem, since the Home Office lacks a sufficient degree of control over B; and, in any case, the harm caused is arguably not reasonably foreseeable—certainly A would not seem to be in a class of persons that was especially at risk from B's actions.

Analysis

Generally

In the cold light of day, this answer may seem 'nothing special', but in the heat of the exam it will require a lot in terms of recall, organization, and application; and in the eyes of the examiner it will stand out as an oasis in a desert—a clear, concise, and authoritative approach to an awkward multi-party problem question. This is not to say that the answer is beyond improvement. No doubt there are all sorts of qualifications or further explanations which one could make, but it is along the right lines: pairing up the parties, identifying the relevant issues, elucidating the relevant rules and principles, applying them to the question so as to reach reasoned conclusions (the 'IRAC method'). For example:

[Parties] Dirk v Alice.

[Issue]   The tort of negligence allows claims to be made for mental as well as physical or
           pecuniary harms (*McLoughlin v O'Brian* (1983, HL); *Alcock* (1992, HL)). Accordingly,
           Dirk (D) may wish to sue A for the nervous shock he sustains as a result of the
           breaking of the jam jars.

[Rules]   It is a requirement that the shock induces some form of psychiatric illness. Broadly, the
           same 'hurdles' that are discussed in the above section of the answer apply (i.e. duty,
           breach, damage). Traditionally the courts have construed the duty of care narrowly in
           the context of nervous shock. According to *White v Chief Constable of South Yorkshire*
           (1998, HL), a person who negligently exposes another to a risk of injury can be held
           liable for any psychological damage this may cause irrespective of whether the threat-
           ened physical injury fails to occur (see also *Dulieu v White* (1901), and *Page v Smith*
           (1995)). The claimant's fear of injury must, however, be reasonable given the nature of
           the risk and the claimant's position: *McFarlane v Wilkinson* (1997, CA).

[Application and conclusion]

           It is unlikely, therefore, that D will be able to bring a successful claim. D is, after all,
           very far away at the time of the incident in question ('at the other end of the store'),
           and it would seem unreasonable, in view of the nature of the risk created, for A to owe
           D a duty of care. Moreover, D merely suffers 'traumatic memories' which may not be
           sufficient to constitute a recognized psychiatric illness. (Compare *Walters v North
           Glamorgan NHS Trust* (2002), where a woman who watched her child die over a
           36-hour period was entitled to damages for nervous shock.)

The point of the answer is not to produce a blueprint for you to follow, but to show, by
example, the way in which you can go about producing an answer which will do justice
to your legal knowledge and enable you to score well in an exam.

Specific points to note

(a) 'Issue identification and structure': Since, as with all legal problems, we are trying to
determine the rights and liabilities of the parties, the answer has focused on the torts
committed by each of the 'actors'. The legal issue here, then, is who is liable in negligence
and to whom?

(b) 'Rule(s) of law': In addition to a good clear structure the answer does not shy away
from outlining the relevant legal rules. In fact the law is set out clearly, using the 'micro
structure' of the 'duty, breach, and damage' formula. Since these elements are relevant to
more than one area of the answer, it is permissible to refer back to some of the principles
you have mentioned earlier if they are in fact pertinent to the discussion you have
embarked upon (for an example of this, see, Dirk v Alice, and Alice v B/HO/S). Most of the
legal rules are supported by authority—over ten cases are cited. The variety of ways in
which these authorities are handled is worth noting. For example, in one instance, the
case is mentioned and then the principle is outlined:

In *Donoghue v Stevenson* (1932, HL), Lord Atkin laid down two principles which determine the
existence of a duty of care: foreseeability and proximity. The test of foreseeability is an objective

one and is based on whether a reasonable person in the defendant's position would have foreseen that his actions would adversely affect others. Proximity refers to whether the defendant would have expected his actions to affect a particular person or class of persons. More recent cases, such as *Caparo v Dickman* (1990, HL), have added an additional limb to this test: the imposition of the duty must be 'fair, just and reasonable' (confirmed by the House of Lords in *Marc Rich v Bishop Rock Marine* (1995)).

Again:

In *The Wagon Mound* (1966, PC) it was held that damages could be recovered only for the type of harm that was reasonably foreseeable.

This may be contrasted with other examples where the principle is outlined and then the authority for the proposition is given:

A must exercise the care of an ordinary person (*Roberts v Ramsbottom* (1980)).

Or:

Next, we must consider whether A's breach was the factual cause of the damage sustained by S (the 'but for' test: *Barnett v Chelsea Hospital*).

It is permissible (and perhaps desirable) to support your proposition of law with more than one authority:

In addition, the courts are reluctant to attribute liability for the acts of third parties (*Smith v Littlewoods* (1987, HL); and *Topp v London Country Bus* (1993, CA)).

Note, also, that legal rules can be stated in the negative:

It is no defence for A to allege that she is shortsighted: *Nettleship v Weston*, where the actions of a learner driver were held to be measured against the standard of an experienced driver.

Lastly, the case can be used as an example of the point the student wishes to make:

The latter's only defence might be to claim that S was contributorily negligent, resulting in a reduced award of damages (Law Reform (Contributory Negligence) Act 1945). An example from the case law is *Capps v Miller*, where a motorcyclist had his damages reduced by 10 per cent for not wearing his helmet.

Note also, how, when dealing with a new topic within the problem, the answer goes from the general to the specific:

The tort of negligence allows claims to be made for mental as well as physical or pecuniary harms (*McLoughlin v O'Brian* (1983, HL)) **[general]**. Accordingly David (D) may wish to sue A in negligence for the nervous shock he sustains as a result of the breaking of the jam jars. It is a requirement that the nervous shock induces some form of psychiatric illness **[specific]**.

The *general* statement helps to locate your new paragraph on the 'legal map', while the *specific* statement gets you to the heart of the problem. Such an approach is both extremely clear and along the right lines for the purposes of presenting your material in terms of legal issues and outlining the relevant rules or principles of law.

(c) 'Application': In addition to issue-spotting and outlining any relevant law, it is necessary for the legal principles you have identified to be applied to the facts. The answer, again, demonstrates this:

> Applying these principles to the problem, it would appear that A falls within this test and hence does owe S a duty of care, since a reasonable person in A's shoes should have been able to foresee that by acting carelessly she might adversely affect others.

Confirmation of this general approach of setting out the law first and then proceeding to apply it to the facts, can readily be found in the law reports. For example, Lord Goff's speech in the House of Lords decision of *Henderson v Merrett Syndicates Ltd* [1994] 3 WLR 761 at 773–778, where his Lordship outlines and extends the principle in *Hedley Byrne v Heller* [1964] AC 465 (dealing with negligent misstatements) (773–777) and then applies it to the facts (777–778). See also Lord Denning's judgment in *Esso Petroleum v Mardon* [1976] 2 All ER 5 at 14–16, CA. And, for an even more obvious example, see Lord Denning's judgment in *Seager v Copydex Ltd* [1967] 2 All ER 415, at 417–418, CA.

Note also that the part of the answer headed 'Alice v Bill' offers a good example of what was referred to in Chapter 1 (on criminal law) as the 'issue within the issue'. Clearly the 'ultimate' issue here is whether Alice can sue Bill, Safeco, or the Home Office for the tort of negligence. However, this is both obvious and easy. What the examiner is really getting at is the 'issue within the issue', i.e. a discussion of some—or one—of the more detailed element(s) that would need to be established in order to determine the 'ultimate' issue. The examiner knows that you will spot and discuss the more obvious points in determining this ultimate issue, but they will understandably want the bulk of your discussion to be directed at some narrower aspect(s) of the problem. Your application of the law to the facts must be sensitive to this point. For example:

> A may sue B in negligence for the injuries she sustains as a result of her collision with the shopping trolley. Again the above principles set out in S v A (above) are relevant **[see the part of the answer dealing with Safeco v Alice]**. It would seem clear that B owes A a duty of care and that the duty has been breached. Equally, it seems clear that 'but for' the breach A would not have sustained her injuries **[that disposes of the more obvious points]**. The crucial issue here, however, seems to be whether the extent of her injuries was foreseeable, in that A suffers from a fragile bone condition of which B did not know. Although in *The Wagon Mound* it was held ...
> **[here attention is focused not on the tort of negligence generally, but on the damage limb, and on only one particular aspect of it]**.

Again, as in criminal law—with *actus reus* and *mens rea*—there is no convention on whether, when applying your material to the facts, you should set out all of the relevant legal principles relating to duty, breach, and damage first and then apply it to the facts, or whether you should set out each limb separately and apply. Much will depend on whether the question has obvious aspects which require little discussion, or whether every element of the tort is contentious. Clearly, if it is obvious that no duty can be established there is little point in discussing breach and damage.

(d) 'Conclusion': The answer argues towards a conclusion in each section. For example:

Safeco v Alice

S would, however, be permitted to claim for consequential loss only, and not for any pure economic loss (*Spartan Steel v Martin*). Thus, S could recover for the £400 worth of jam and for the cost of cleaning it up. However, S could not claim for the profits lost as a result of turning away customers while cleaning up, or for the profits lost because Dirk does not shop there anymore.

Sometimes (e.g. where the defendant has a defence) your conclusion will need to take account of defensive strategies. Again, as with criminal law, it is appropriate that defensive strategies are discussed only after having identified liability creating factors:

The latter's only defence might be to claim that S was contributorily negligent, resulting in a reduced award of damages (Law Reform (Contributory Negligence) Act 1945). An example from the case law is *Capps v Miller*, where a motorcyclist had his damages reduced by 10 per cent for not wearing his helmet. On the facts of the problem question, there is a good argument that S is to some degree responsible for its own misfortunes by virtue of the fact that it stacks, in the form of a pyramid, easily breakable jars near the entrance to the supermarket.

2   Occupiers' liability and the Animals Act 1971

Negligence liability in *Donoghue v Stevenson* and its progeny is concerned with establishing a common law duty of care in certain circumstances (e.g. nervous shock, negligent misstatement, and so on). By contrast, in relation to occupier's liability, a specific duty of care is imposed by statute. Consequently, occupier's liability can be considered as a special type of negligence liability, governed by its own special rules.

Although liability for damage caused by animals can be established on the basis of ordinary tort principles (e.g. common law negligence), this is another area where statute law is particularly important (see the Animals Act 1971). The following question highlights these issues.

Question

Jack owns a derelict plot of land which he intends to develop when market conditions are suitable. He has erected a fence around the site, upon which he has placed notices stating: 'Private property. Keep out. Anyone entering these premises does so at their own risk. All liability for any damage is hereby excluded.'

Local children have for some time been entering the plot through a large gap in the fence in order to play. Kylie, aged 10, was playing hide and seek on the plot when she sustained serious injuries as a result of falling through a rusted manhole cover which is obscured by undergrowth.

Following this incident Jack had the fence repaired. He allowed a stray mongrel dog to wander around the plot and fed it regularly. He hoped that the presence of the dog would deter intruders. He placed additional notices on the fence stating 'Beware of the Dog'. Lenny, aged 17, was playing football near the fence when the ball was accidentally kicked over the fence onto Jack's land. Lenny climbed over the fence to retrieve the ball and was savagely attacked by the dog.

Discuss.

Suggested answer

Jack's liability to Kylie

Jack (J) may owe (and be in breach of) a duty of care to Kylie (K) under the Occupiers' Liability Act 1957 (OLA 1957) or 1984 (OLA 1984). Since the duties created by both Acts are owed by 'occupiers', it must be shown that J fulfils this requirement. The test for 'occupier' (a term which is not defined by either statute) is 'occupational control', though control does not have to be exclusive (*Wheat v E Lacon* (1966, HL)). Given that J owns the plot of land and intends to develop it (he has control over it), he is covered by the legislation. Meanwhile, the term 'premises' is defined widely in s 1(3), OLA 1957, to cover land and movable and immovable structures. Since J owns and is in control of the land, and all therein, including the rusted manhole cover—which might constitute a movable structure—there is a good argument to suggest that he occupies premises.

OLA 1957—Assuming K is a visitor

For a duty to be owed under the OLA 1957 it must be established that K was a 'visitor', i.e. a person who either (i) has the express permission of the occupier to visit the premises, or (ii) can be said to have an implied permission to be there (s 1(1), OLA 1957). Although K does not have permission to be on the land as such, the law has generally been sympathetic to children in occupier's liability cases. At common law, a child could be upgraded to a visitor if there was either an allurement or an implied licence. For there to be an allurement there must have been something on the land that was both 'fascinating and fatal' (*Glasgow Corporation v Taylor* (1922)). Given that the plot was derelict—save for the undergrowth—there would not appear to be an allurement. For there to have been an implied licence, it must be shown that J was aware of child trespassers and had taken no steps to keep them out: *Lowery v Walker* (1911, HL). J should have been aware that children had, for some time, been entering the land and playing. The fact that there was a large gap in the fence, which had not been mended, could be enough to establish an implied licence (contrast the position in *Edwards v Railway Executive* (1952), where the defendant company had sought to repair a fence that had a hole in it). On this basis, K could be deemed to be a visitor. The duty owed by J to K is a duty to ensure that K is not injured by reason of the state of the premises (*Fairchild v Glenhaven Funeral Services Ltd* (2002, CA)). There is an argument that injury to K results from the existence of a hidden danger—the rusted manhole which is obscured by undergrowth—and that, accordingly, J is in breach of his duty to keep K safe.

Although an occupier has, in theory, a number of defences available to a claim brought by a visitor under the OLA 1957. Whether the warning 'Keep Out . . .' constitutes sufficient notice or amounts to consent by K (s 2(5), OLA 1957) is debatable given that K is only 10.

OLA 1984—Assuming K is a trespasser

If K is deemed by the law not to have an implied licence to be on the land (as is entirely plausible), she will be viewed as a trespasser and therefore will be unable to rely on the OLA 1957. However, J may be liable under the OLA 1984 which applies to 'non-visitors', e.g. trespasses: s 1(1)(a), OLA

1984 ('occupies', 'premises' are defined as above). According to s 1(3) of the Act, J owes a statutory duty of care to non-visitors if:

(a) he is aware of the danger or has reasonable grounds to believe that it exists (*Tomlinson v Congleton* (2003, HL)); and

(b) he knows or has reasonable grounds to believe that a non-visitor is in the vicinity of the danger; and

(c) the risk is one which reasonably requires the non-visitor to receive some protection (*Donoghue v Folkstone Properties* (2003, CA)—the defendants had no grounds to believe that anyone would try to dive into the harbour, as it was in the middle of winter).

It is unclear from the facts whether J was aware of the danger or he knew or had reason to believe that non-visitors were in the vicinity. However, it could be argued that the fact that J puts up a notice and erects a fence suggests that he does recognize the existence of some risk, and that he is aware that non-visitors are in the vicinity. The notice and the fence *may* have been his response to this knowledge (compare *Swain v Natui Ram Puri* (1996), where the Court of Appeal held that there was no reason to believe that children would climb on to the defendant's roof). If J knew there was a hole in the fence it would be very difficult for him to deny the existence of a duty under s 1(3). Certainly the risk—a hidden danger—is of the type that one might reasonably expect would require the non-visitor to receive some protection.

If J is deemed to owe a duty, then he must take such care as is reasonable in all the circumstances of the case to ensure that the non-visitor does not suffer injury as a result of the danger in question: s 1(4) (i.e. this is an issue which relates to the *standard* of care owed). Although there is some degree of doubt as to the exact nature of the test to be applied, it seems reasonable to assume that the court will demand a higher standard of care from a public corporation than from a homeowner. Factors taken into account when determining reasonable care include:

(a) the seriousness and probability of injury—the greater the risk, the greater the precautions needed;

(b) the nature of the premises;

(c) the degree to which it was foreseeable that the non-visitor would enter them.

It would seem highly foreseeable that children will enter a derelict plot and that they could injure themselves, albeit not seriously. A hidden danger—as in the problem—would increase the probability of injury, and therefore require that J take greater precautions. J's premises are in a bad state. The fence is in need of repair and parts of the plot are overgrown, giving rise to a greater chance of the existence of hidden dangers. It would seem, therefore, that J has not discharged his duty of care.

In certain circumstances, however, an occupier can discharge his duty by taking reasonable steps to (i) give a warning; and (ii) discourage non-visitors from incurring the risk (s 1(5)). The notice would probably not suffice as a warning—something more would be needed. In any case, where the victim is a child (as here; K is only 10) a warning is unlikely to be enough. Although J fenced off the area, the fencing is defective, and therefore it is extremely unlikely that his attempts to negate liability would be successful. In addition, the failure to maintain the fence is probably the cause of K's injuries (distinguishing *Titchner* (1983, HL)).

According to s 1(6), the occupier will not be liable where the non-visitor voluntarily assumes the risk. Since K is only 10, a plausible argument can be made that she is still a child and thus not capable of appreciating the risk. The same argument would probably apply in relation to the defence of contributory negligence.

The OLA 1984 makes no reference to the issue of whether an occupier can exclude or restrict potential liability under the Act. If it is possible to exclude all duties (on the basis that all duties can be excluded unless statute says otherwise) then subject to common law rules (e.g. *contra proferentem*, where any ambiguity will be construed against the party seeking to rely on the exclusion clause) J will not be held to be liable to K. However, it could be that no duties may be excluded (or only some, e.g. it may not be possible to exclude the 'minimal' common law duties owed to trespassers by virtue of *Herrington* (1972, HL)), in which case J would have to place heavy reliance on s 1(5) and (6) as defences. This is a very unclear area and the whole issue of whether it is possible to exclude one's duties remains an open question.

If J's duty can be excluded, the protections offered by the UCTA 1977 do not apply, since s 1(1), UCTA deals only with the exclusion of liability for common law negligence and the duty owed under OLA 1957. It is worth noting that the absence of any mention of the OLA 1984 in s 1(1), UCTA 1977 would tend to support the argument that Parliament intended the OLA 1984 duty to be non-excludable.

J's liability to Lenny (L)

J may be liable to pay compensation to L under the Animals Act 1971. In accordance with the requirements of s 2(2), liability can be imposed on anyone who *keeps* an animal which belongs to a *non-dangerous species*. A mongrel dog would be classified as a non-dangerous species, since it is an animal commonly domesticated in the British Isles (s 6(2)). J is liable as keeper if he owns the dog or has it in his possession (s 6(3)). Since he feeds the stray, this would probably be enough to bring him within the section, but in any case he has the dog fenced in, so clearly he has it in his possession. According to s 2(2), three requirements need to be satisfied. First, that the damage was of a kind which the animal was likely to cause (a guard dog is likely to be aggressive unless restrained—contrast *Gloster v Chief Constable of Greater Manchester Police* (2000), involving a *trained* police dog). Secondly, the likelihood of the damage was due to special characteristics of the animal which are not normally found in animals of the same species (dogs are usually non-aggressive unless threatened). And thirdly, liability ensues if the keeper has actual knowledge—constructive knowledge will not suffice—that the dog had characteristics that would render it dangerous. On this last point, there is little to indicate that J knew that the dog had any aggressive characteristics: he 'hoped' that it would deter intruders. The sign merely says 'Beware of the Dog', and not 'Beware: *Dangerous* Dog'. We are not told if the dog has previously attacked. On the other hand, J was using the dog as a guard dog, and a guard dog which was not aggressive would be pointless.

Even if s 2(2) is satisfied, J will have a defence if the injury was wholly L's fault (s 5(1)). If it was partly L's fault, then an issue of contributory negligence applies—see Law Reform (Contributory Negligence) Act 1945, ss 10 and 11. J will also escape liability, if L has assumed the risk (s 5(2)), or if it was reasonable to keep the dog for the purpose of protecting property (s 5(3)) (this subsection applies only if L is a trespasser, which would have to be established). It is arguable that all these defences apply: L is, after all, 17 and should know better (see *Cummings v Granger* (1977, CA)). However, s 5(3) should now be construed in the light of the Guard Dogs Act 1975 (given that J has almost certainly committed a criminal offence under that Act, it is unlikely that a court would hold that what he has done is reasonable for the purposes of s 5(3)).

If J does not fall within s 2(2), then he may be liable on the basis of ordinary negligence principles. **[Discuss the tort of negligence: duty, breach, and damage]**.

Analysis

(a) Again, at a general level, the answer is supported by a good, clear, tight structure: who may sue whom, and for what. Under each heading the relevant tort(s) is/are identified and the appropriate rules are set out. Subsequently, the rules are applied to the facts to reach credible conclusions in the light of possible defences and/or mitigating factors.

(b) The question requires students to make good use of their *statutory* material by clearly setting out, and subsequently applying, the relevant law to the relevant facts. However, although the approach is essentially the same as that suggested for common law material, there are nonetheless specific difficulties worth looking out for. Since statutory material can often be complex, you should try to see whether it is possible to summarize the provision(s) in a line or two, by capturing the *essence* of the liability involved. An example of this in the answer can be found in relation to the Animals Act 1971:

> And thirdly, liability ensues if the keeper has actual knowledge—constructive knowledge will not suffice—that the dog had characteristics that would render it dangerous.

Having something like this to write down will prevent you from becoming swamped by the complexity of the statutory provision(s) and will demonstrate to the examiner that you have been able to manipulate the material. Of course you do not have to formulate this sort of synthesis yourself, the textbook writers provide many examples of how this may be done.

It may, however, not be possible to reduce the complexity of a key statutory provision to a single sentence: e.g. s 1(3), OLA 1984. Nonetheless, in the answer, every effort has been made to simplify the subsection by paraphrasing its essential elements (see also Chapter 1, p 14 dealing with s 2, Homicide Act 1957 (diminished responsibility)).

(c) The common law is not excluded unless a statute uses words that point to that conclusion. Therefore in many legal textbooks and articles the common law position on a particular issue is often considered first, with the statutory position being overlaid.[2] However, in an exam context—where time is a precious commodity—such an approach is often dangerous. In such circumstances it might be more sensible to set out the most relevant body of law first before considering the common law position. In the above question, although the common law has some relevance, the Act provides extensive coverage for occupiers' liability and it is only in a 'filling in the gaps' sense that a discussion of the common law would really be necessary (e.g. in relation to 'occupiers', or in relation to excluding duties). However, you do not need to discuss the common law

---

2. But note, although the statute might *not* have the effect of abrogating the common law on a particular issue, the fact that the statutory regime is often clearer and less cumbersome may mean that *in practice* there is little need to resort to the common law.

position at all if it has in fact been totally overridden by statutory developments; or if the direction at the end of the question is along the lines of: 'Discuss, with reference to the Occupiers' Liability Acts'.

3 *Rylands v Fletcher*/nuisance/negligence

Question

Alan operates a factory in Bristown in which he manufactures computer components. For the purposes of this work Alan keeps a stock of metal foil at one end of the factory. As a result of the door of the factory being left open, some of the foil is blown out of the factory by a gust of wind. It lands on an electricity pylon owned by Branson Electrical Supplies plc, damages the pylon, and causes a power cut in the area.

Celia operates a factory next door to Alan which manufactures plastic gnomes. When the power is cut off the production line ceases to operate and the electrical furnaces which process the plastic go off, cool, and have to be cleaned out. The power remains off for the next 48 hours. Celia claims to have lost £10,000 profits as a result of these occurrences.

Delia, who was riding her moped past the factory at the time the foil was blown out, was struck by some foil, crashed the moped, and was killed.
Discuss.

Suggested answer

Alan's liability to Branson

Rylands v Fletcher. Alan (A) could be liable to Branson (B) by virtue of the rule in *Rylands v Fletcher*. This is a strict liability tort (i.e. if the elements of the tort are satisfied it is irrelevant that the defendant has taken reasonable care to avoid the damage caused—albeit that certain elements seem to have a reasonableness component). Compensation for physical damage (as here) is covered by *Rylands*. The tort is not confined to claims between adjacent landowners (*Charing Cross v Hydraulic Power* (1913, CA)). There is English authority to suggest that even a non-occupier who has no interest in the land of any kind can invoke the rule (*British Celanese v Hunt* (1969), where damage occurred on a third party's land). Thus, the fact that B is not an adjacent freeholder is irrelevant for the purposes of liability. B has a prima facie claim, even though it appears merely to have an interest in the pylons on the land, rather than in the land itself.

An action in *Rylands v Fletcher* will arise where there has been (i) an escape; (ii) of something dangerous; (iii) which has been brought on to the land; and (iv) which has a non-natural use. 'Escape' for the purposes of liability in *Rylands* means 'escape from a place where the defendant has occupation or control over land to a place where it is outside his occupation or control' (*Read v J Lyons* (1947) *per* Lord Simon). The dangerous 'thing' must have been brought on to the land. The occupier will not be liable for anything naturally on the land (so, e.g. landslides and other naturally occurring phenomena are not covered). Applying this to the facts, there has been an escape: foil from A's factory (which was in his possession or control) has moved to a place where it is outside his control. The 'thing' (the foil) is not naturally occurring; instead it has been brought to and kept on the land.

Whether there has been an escape of something that is 'dangerous' and has a 'non-natural' use is, however, problematic. In the recent House of Lords decision in *Transco* (2003), their Lordships viewed these two requirements as interlinked and stipulated that they were to be determined by 'ordinary contemporary standards'. According to Lord Bingham there has to be an 'exceptionally high risk of danger'. Moreover, the activity must be highly unusual or 'special' to warrant strict liability (*per* Lord Walker). Their Lordships resorted to the test of reasonable foreseeability in determining whether an activity was dangerous and unusual. The question of whether the use of the land was of benefit to the local community, and adopted in earlier cases such as *Rickards v Lothian* (1913, PC), was no longer seen as relevant.

Applying the above principles to the facts, A must surely have known, or had at his disposal the means of knowing (e.g. his employees could have told him), that the foil had dangerous propensities were it not properly stored. Common sense would indicate this; the harm is therefore foreseeable. In *British Celanese v A H Hunt* (a case on similar facts to those in the problem) it was held that the manufacture of electric components on an industrial estate did not constitute a non-natural use. Here, however, there is no suggestion that A's factory is on an industrial estate, pointing to the conclusion that there is a non-natural use. That said, the quantity of foil, and the purpose and manner of its storage, would need to be ascertained before a more reliable conclusion could be drawn (*Mason v Levy Auto Parts* (1967)).

Nuisance: A could also be liable to B in nuisance. An action in private nuisance is defined by Winfield & Jolowicz as 'an unlawful interference with a person's use or enjoyment of land, or some right over, or in connection with it' (adopted with approval in *Read v Lyons* (1945, CA) *per*, Scott LJ). Traditionally, two types of interference are recognized as being capable of giving rise to an action in nuisance (*St Helen's Smelting Co v Tipping* (1865, HL)):

(a) interferences with P's beneficial use of the premises (e.g. excessive noise: *Christie v Davey* (1893)); basically, the idea here is that the interference should substantially detract from P's comfort or enjoyment in the use of her premises; or

(b) physical damage to the premises or to P's property situated on the premises, e.g. causing damage to P's land.

By leaving the factory door open, and thus allowing the foil to be blown out of the factory, A would appear to be responsible for an interference with B's enjoyment of the premises and physical damage to those premises. The foil interferes with B's beneficial use of its pylon (i.e. to make profits; pursue its business interests, etc.); and the foil also causes physical damage to B's pylon (in fact this would probably be the better ground upon which to proceed).

Not every interference is actionable—people must tolerate a certain degree of interference. Instead, it must be shown that the interference was unreasonable. Reasonableness is a question of fact. This is relatively straightforward where the interference results in physical damage to property (as here). Where, however, the interference relates to the enjoyment of the land, the claimant must prove substantial interference, so as to affect the reasonable person's comfort.

Even if there has been an unlawful interference, B may not have a sufficient legal interest in the land to allow it to sue. However, in line with modern authorities on this issue (e.g. *Khorasandjian v Bush* (1993, CA)—judicial willingness to accommodate an interest on the basis of any type of occupation or possession), it would seem that in all likelihood B does have a sufficient legal interest in the land (cf *Hunter v Canary Wharf* (1997), where the Court of Appeal ruled that loss of a recreational facility was insufficient interference to ground an action in nuisance).

Assuming B's action is successful it will be able to claim damages for any loss which is reasonably foreseeable (*The Wagon Mound (No 2)* (1967, PC)). Therefore, in addition to the repair of the damaged property, business losses which result from the fact that the pylon has been damaged by the nuisance are recoverable (e.g. *Andreae v Selfridge* (1938, CA), in which losses caused to hotel owner as a result of a nuisance were calculated by way of lost custom).

Negligence: Liability may also arise in negligence **[discuss, in particular, whether there is a duty of care—difficult to argue foreseeability or proximity]**.

Alan's liability to Celia

Ordinarily economic losses are not recoverable under *Rylands*. Thus, Celia (C) will only be able to sue under *Rylands* if there was actual physical damage to her furnaces—though economic losses consequential on this physical damage are seemingly recoverable: *Cambridge Water* (1994, HL).

Liability may, however, arise in negligence, if it can be shown that A owed a duty to C (which would involve foreseeability of harm to her) and that A breached that duty (by falling below the standard of the reasonable factory owner) in such a way as to cause C loss. Nonetheless, there is still the problem of what damage C has suffered. If property damage can be established, C can recover for that damage and for any consequential economic loss (*Spartan Steel* (1973)). If the loss is purely economic, the law is reluctant to allow recovery (*AMEC Civil Engeering* (1997)).

A's liability to Delia

Rylands v Fletcher: Until the recent House of Lords decision in *Transco* it was unclear whether a plaintiff could claim for personal injuries under the rule in *Rylands v Fletcher*. In *Transco*, their Lordships affirmed that *Rylands* was a sub-species of nuisance which protected rights to and enjoyment of land. Claims for personal injury and death (as here) are, therefore, excluded.

Either negligence or public nuisance **[Discuss (briefly) either negligence (see *Hilder v Assoc Portland Cement* [1961] 1 WLR 1434—football escaped into road knocking motorcyclist off—but unlikely), or public nuisance or both.**

Analysis

(a) It is clear from the answer that the issues here involve liability in *Rylands*, nuisance, and negligence (note that liability in negligence is capable of cropping up almost anywhere in a tort exam). Although the answer could have been structured on the basis of the issues/torts, again a split along 'party lines' was preferred. Had the issues/torts approach been adopted the flow of the answer would have looked like this:

Liability in Rylands v Fletcher
Alan's liability to Branson
    Ingredients of the tort
    Application to facts relating to A v B
    Conclusion

Alan's liability to Celia

Apply the above ingredients to reach a conclusion

Alan's liability to Delia

Apply the above ingredients to reach a conclusion

Liability in negligence

Alan's liability to Branson

Ingredients: duty, breach, damage

Application

Conclusion

Alan's liability to Celia

Apply the above ingredients to reach a conclusion

Alan's liability to Delia

Apply the above ingredients to reach a conclusion

Liability in nuisance

Alan's liability to Branson

Ingredients of the tort

Application to facts relating to A v B

Conclusion

Alan's liability to Delia

Apply the above ingredients to reach a conclusion

Although under this structure you would minimize repetition of the relevant principles, it requires more of an 'aerial' view of the question, demanding more of you than the chronological/parties approach which has been heavily utilized by us. Nonetheless, it is a useful method and, if done properly, will allow you to score good marks.

(b) The key elements which need to be shown are set out. Unlike with criminal law, you will notice that many of the ingredients of the torts alleged are unclear. This fact may be frustrating, but it need not be problematic from the point of view of sitting an exam. Lack of clarity is to be embraced, since it will provide you with more 'grist for your (exam) mill'. For example, in relation to the meaning of 'dangerous' and 'non-natural use' there is a lack of precision as to exactly what these terms mean. Although the conclusion is reached that there is a non-natural use of the land, this conclusion is sensibly qualified by a request for more information as to the quantity of the foil and the manner of its storage.

(c) You will note that there are a number of 'issue within the issue' points—for example, in discussing A's liability to C (in *Rylands*). Here, your focus ought not to be on establishing all the ingredients for a claim under *Rylands* (which have in any case been discussed earlier in the answer), but on the nature of the damages that may be claimed. Similarly, in addressing A's liability to D, it would be wasted economy (especially given the other issues raised by the question) to establish that D's estate had a prima facie claim against A under *Rylands* if the tort does not extend to providing compensation for death or personal injuries.

4 Summary

- Self-standing, or nominate, torts have their own specific ingredients (albeit that some of these are unclear and evolving) in much the same way that different crimes have their own *actus reus* and *mens rea* ingredients. Likewise, these torts have applicable defences just as crimes have applicable defences.

- Make sure you have distinguished clearly in your mind the difference between these types of torts and issues like vicarious liability. The latter form of liability does not represent a distinct tort. Instead it is a means by which some person can be held liable for the torts committed by another. It is a means of displacing liability from one person to another (e.g. from the employee to the employer).

- Remember, negligence is not only a self-standing tort—the tort of negligence—but may also be relevant to the way in which other torts are committed (e.g. nuisance); it is also a way in which certain contracts can be breached.

- Although the number of relevant authorities cited in your answer is important, the way in which you introduce and sideline or distinguish case law is also important, since it gives an air of sophistication to your answers.

- Learning from the techniques employed in marshalling authorities in the various answers above is no substitute for actually reading cases and observing how judges and barristers manipulate case law and statutory provisions.

- Although textbooks often set out the common law position first before considering statutory developments, such an approach is not always appropriate with respect to problem questions. This is especially so where the common law has been abrogated by the statute law; or where statutory developments leave very little room for the common law to operate.

- Unlike with criminal law, you will notice that many of the ingredients of the torts alleged are unclear. This fact may be frustrating, but it need not be problematic from the point of view of sitting an exam. In fact, exploring the various possibilities provides you with more 'grist for your (exam) mill'.

3 The law of contract

As with the previous chapter, the purpose here is to apply the problem-solving approach outlined in Chapter 1 and developed in Chapter 2—this time to specific areas of contract law. In doing so, we again provide 'micro structures' around which to present answers. As before, we are interested in identifying legal issues, outlining the relevant law and applying it to the facts so as to reach reasoned conclusions. However, while the same techniques as outlined earlier in this book are broadly applicable, there are some signifi-cant differences in emphasis. Unlike criminal law and tort law, there are no longer easily definable categories of offences/torts and defences to provide 'ready-made' frameworks around which to build answers. Thus contract law problems require us to modify slightly the problem-solving method we have so far employed. In this respect it will be helpful to pay particular attention to the following points:

(a) Generally, the first step in any contract question is to discover whether a contract exists, since an understanding of the legal issues stems from the existence of a contract. Some questions specifically focus on the issue of formation (e.g. the first two questions in this chapter). In other questions, however, it is patently clear that a contract has been formed. Where this is so, the examiner is really interested in issues relating to, say, the extent of the obligations owed by the parties and the performance of the contract (e.g. a question on exemption clauses, or frustration, or breach of contract). On other occasions, the contract will again already have been formed, but the legal issue(s) may relate, for example, to statements made before the formation of the contract which have induced one party to enter into it (as with misrepresentation). The point is: the existence of a contract is central to all contract questions, albeit that it is not the *focus* of all contract questions. Consequently, you do not need to waste time on issues relating to formation of the contract if it is clear that one exists and no-one would care to dispute it.

(b) Insofar as there is a key with which to 'unlock' contract problem questions, it lies in addressing the various *statements* (written and oral) made by the different parties in the question posed. It is important, therefore, that you are able to categorize and assess the contractual significance of these statements and to outline any accompanying remedies. The first question below, about Zoe—involving contract formation—provides a good example of this process at work, as does the question about Rod (p 67). The above suggestion—that you should concentrate on statements—ought not to be construed too narrowly. The statements must be considered in their context: the status of the parties (i.e. their bargaining positions); the setting—formal or informal (e.g. after a long night of drinking and frivolity); the expressions or gestures of the parties; and so on.

(c) As we have already seen, all problem questions involve assessing the *rights/liabilities/obligations/duties of the parties*. For example: what does X want, and from whom, and how will X get it? If you start *thinking* in this way you will not go far wrong. In contract law, providing answers to questions such as these will require the identification of a contractual doctrine upon which X may rely (e.g. the doctrine of common mistake), or a legal principle derived from a case (e.g. *Williams v Roffey*), or derived from a statutory provision (such as the Unfair Contract Terms Act 1977). Not only will you need to identify the particular legal doctrine, principle, etc. that X aims to rely upon, but you will also need to explain fully why it is applicable on the facts.

The topics covered in this chapter include formation, exclusion clauses, misrepresentation, and mistake.

1 Formation

Questions on contract formation are standard fare in contract law exams. While conceptually they are usually straightforward, they are often 'bitty' and structuring your answer can at times be problematic.

Question

Zoe, a young ballerina with no head for business, needs £150 urgently to pay a bill. On Tuesday evening she discusses her problem with some friends, Julia and Kathleen. Julia suggests that she sell a valuable pair of antique ballet shoes that she recently inherited from her great aunt, a famous ballerina. 'All right,' says Zoe, 'I'm willing to sell them to either of you for £150. But you'd better post me a written acceptance by Friday morning.'

On Wednesday, Zoe meets Julia in the supermarket. Julia tells Zoe that she would like to buy the shoes, but has to talk to her father first, and that he is abroad until the weekend. 'Oh,' says Zoe, 'forget about that, there's no rush. Just give me a ring some time.'

On Thursday, Julia unexpectedly receives a large cheque from a fond uncle. She rings Zoe, but gets no reply. So she immediately goes round to Zoe's flat and puts a note through the door which reads, 'I accept your offer of the shoes. Herewith a cheque for £150.'

On the same day, Kathleen posts a letter to Zoe purportedly accepting the offer. But it is delayed in the post and arrives on Saturday.

On Saturday, Zoe discovers that the ballet shoes are worth £1,000.
Advise Zoe.

Suggested answer

Issue I: Offer or invitation to treat?

Any obligation Zoe might have to hand over the shoes will stem from the existence of a contract which she has entered into. It will therefore need to be shown that what Zoe said constitutes an 'offer'. According to *Treitel*, an offer is 'an expression of willingness to contract on specified terms, made with the intention that it shall become binding as soon as it is accepted', i.e. the offeror must be prepared to implement his or her promise should the other person decide to hold him or her to it. The test is objective (*The Hannah Blumenthal* (1983, HL)), so there may still be a contract if, objectively speaking, the parties can be said to have agreed, even though there was not an express agreement. Where there is evidence that the person merely intends to start negotiations which may result in an agreement, s/he is said to make an 'invitation to treat'. So, for example, the display of goods in a shop window (*Fisher v Bell* (1961)) or on the shelves of a self-service shop (*Pharmaceutical Society of GB v Boots* (1953, CA)) is merely an invitation to treat—in such cases the customer is deemed to make the offer. In Zoe's case, the words 'I am willing to sell to you . . .' could, objectively speaking, be construed as an offer, since they indicate a willingness to be bound by certain terms as opposed to an attempt to start negotiations. In addition, she specifies the terms of the acceptance (written acceptance by Friday morning), even though certain aspects of the acceptance remain unclear (e.g. whether she will sell to the first to reply, or to the one who makes the highest offer).

Issue II: Does Zoe enter into a contract with Julia?

According to *Treitel* an acceptance is 'a final and unqualified expression of assent to the terms of an offer', which must be communicated to the offeror (*Holwell Securities v Hughes* (1974, CA)).

One possible interpretation of the events at the supermarket is that Julia makes a conditional acceptance of Zoe's offer (conditional on her father's agreement). On this basis there would be a contract and Zoe would be under an obligation to part with the ballet shoes. Yet such an interpretation seems strained and, objectively speaking, it is unlikely that a contract has been formed.

Another possible interpretation of what happens when Julia meets Zoe at the supermarket, is that what Julia says constitutes a counter-offer and thus a rejection of Zoe's original offer (*Hyde v Wrench*). This would have the effect of terminating the original offer (*Tinn v Hoffmann*) and would thus deny Julia the opportunity of accepting it. As a result, when Julia takes the letter and cheque round to Zoe's house, and slips them under the door, this amounts to the counter-offer, which Zoe is free to accept or reject. However, this interpretation also seems unlikely to be accepted. The conversation between Julia and Zoe will be construed in its context—which was informal—and therefore it is unlikely that a court would say a counter-offer has been made by Julia.

Yet another interpretation of events is that Zoe has either made a new offer or she has varied the terms of acceptance of the initial offer ('Oh, forget about that . . . give me a ring sometime'). Either option could apply to Julia, but not to Kathleen since she has received no notification. If there has been a new offer then Julia's acceptance must be by telephone. With instantaneous communications, acceptance must be received: *Entores v Miles* 1955, CA. This has not occurred. If Zoe has merely varied the terms of acceptance, the issue then is whether or not Julia's note and cheque still constitute a valid acceptance—i.e. does the variation oust the initial terms of the offer or merely supplement them? If it ousts them then Julia will not have made a valid acceptance, since no-one answers her phone call. If, however, Zoe's words in the supermarket are merely intended to supplement the means of accepting the original offer then there is an argument for saying that a binding contract exists between Zoe and Julia. Although the written communication has not arrived by Royal Mail, what Julia has done amounts to the same thing. Therefore Zoe will have to sell the shoes to Julia.

Issue III: Did Kathleen make a valid acceptance?

As a general rule, acceptance takes place when it is brought to the attention of the offeror (here Zoe): *Entores*. However, where the postal rule applies, communication of the acceptance is deemed to have occurred on posting: *Adams v Lindsell*. On this reading, the fact that Kathleen's letter is delayed would be irrelevant: *Household Fire Insurance v Grant* (contract was deemed to be in existence even though posted acceptance never arrived). Therefore a contract would have been formed between Zoe and Kathleen. However, on the facts, it is unclear whether the postal rule actually does apply or whether it has been ousted, as in *Holwell*. Either interpretation is plausible. However, it is submitted that by using the words 'post me a written acceptance by Friday morning', Zoe demonstrates an intention to oust the postal rule (as in *Holwell*). If this is correct, then Kathleen's acceptance comes too late.

Issue IV: Can Zoe revoke her 'offer'?

If Julia has accepted Zoe's offer, Zoe cannot revoke it: *Payne v Cave*. Zoe will therefore have to go ahead with the agreement or suffer the consequences of her breach of contract. Although an award of damages is the usual contractual remedy, the court may in this instance—owing to the unique value and special interest of the goods in question—make an order for specific performance, requiring the defaulting party (here, Zoe) to carry out her contractual obligations.

Issue V: Will the contract with Julia be void for mistake?

Zoe could try to argue that she and Julia have contracted on the basis of a common mistake (that there is some misapprehension about some aspect of the subject matter of the contract—here, that the ballet shoes were so valuable). Shared mistakes as to quality are rarely operative at common law (*Bell v Lever Bros* (1931, HL)). It is unlikely therefore that the contract will be declared void. Although it had previously been said that equity takes a more flexible view of shared fundamental mistakes relating to quality (*Solle v Butcher* (1950); *Grist v Bailey*—where rescission was granted), this view has been rejected by the Court of Appeal in *The Great Peace*.

Conclusion

Failing a satisfactory remedy under the law on mistake, Zoe's best line of defence is to claim either:

(a) that what she said about the shoes was an invitation to treat and not an offer, or

(b) that she did not intend to create legal relations.

Alternatively, she could ask her friends to release her from any legal obligations into which she has entered.

Analysis

What is so special about this answer? On the one hand, there is nothing special about the answer at all. Nothing, that is, that could not be gleaned from a basic textbook outlining the law on offer and acceptance. Certainly there is nothing original about it, neither is everything that could have been drawn out of the question addressed. For example, given that the parties were all friends, perhaps the issue of 'intention to create legal relations' should have been given more weight. However, notwithstanding certain weaknesses, this answer was awarded a very high mark. Why?

Well, there are a number of reasons, and many of them relate back to the suggestions we have already discussed in earlier chapters:

- most of the relevant legal issues have been identified (invitation to treat/offer/acceptance/ revocation/intention to create legal relations/mistake);

- the answer is well structured (i.e. the issues are clearly presented) making the material easy to follow and thus easier to mark than answers which are loaded with material but which are structured awkwardly;

- the law is more than adequately set out and is often accompanied by supporting authority, which is comprehensively yet succinctly applied. Although the analysis is not particularly deep, alternative lines of argument (i.e. different interpretations of the events) are explored; and

- the answer argues towards a conclusion, in particular it does not forget to follow the instruction given, which is to advise Zoe. In fact, in the very last sentence, a practical remedy is even offered.

All in all, the answer represents a significant achievement in terms of recall, organization, and analysis, within the short period of 45 minutes.

In answering the next question a similar type of issues-based structure is presented.

Question

Nicky, an interior decorator, and Simon, a friend who is a builder, are both hit hard by the recession and have time on their hands. Nicky needs a new wall built at the end of her garden. Simon needs some new curtains for his drawing room. Simon tells Nicky that he is happy to build her the wall if she will make up some curtains for him 'in return'. Nicky agrees and Simon starts work on the wall.

One day when Simon is working, Nicky's neighbour Jo pops in for a coffee. She admires Simon's work, and asks him if he could come round later to fit a new lock to her door. Simon agrees, and later that day fits the lock. Jo is so pleased that she promises to send Simon £50.

The next day Simon receives an offer of immediate temporary employment from a local builder. He tells Nicky that he can only finish the wall if she pays him £250 for the work. Nicky agrees, and Simon turns down the job and finishes the wall.

Now both Nicky and Jo are refusing to pay Simon anything.
Advise Simon.

Suggested answer

For a bilateral contract to be enforceable there must exist: (i) an agreement (which can be evidenced by an 'offer' and an 'acceptance'); (ii) an intention to create legal relations; and (iii) a set of promises—forming the basis of the contract—which are 'supported' by consideration.

Issue I: Does the initial agreement between Simon and Nicky constitute an enforceable contract?

Notwithstanding signs of a bargain (doing something in return for something), the crucial question here is whether Simon (S) and Nicky (N) intended to create legal relations. Commercial agreements are presumed to do so; however, for social and domestic agreements, the presumption is reversed (*Balfour v Balfour*: agreement to pay spouse £30 per week was unenforceable). While this presumption is not easy to rebut, it is still possible. For example, *Jones v Padavatton* (1969, CA) is authority for the proposition that if agreements have a serious impact on the lives of family members, it is more likely that there was an intention to create legal relations (see also *Errington v Errington* (1952, CA)).

Applying these principles to the facts, it would appear that there was no intention to create legal relations, since this is a social arrangement falling within *Balfour* (N and S are friends). Although the presumption established in *Balfour* can be rebutted, it is unlikely that this has occurred. The language and context of the arrangement (they have time on their hands and are both hard hit by the recession) points towards an agreement which is not legally binding. This conclusion is, however, by no means certain.

Issue II: Is Jo's promise to pay Simon £50 binding on her?

Determining whether Jo's (J) promise to pay Simon (S) £50 is binding upon her, hinges on whether it was supported by consideration. The requirement of consideration is recognition by the law that contracts should ordinarily involve some form of bargain or exchange. In addition, consideration must be sufficient (i.e. it must have some value in the eyes of the law), though it need not be adequate (*Chappell v Nestle* (1960, HL)). The consideration must also have moved from the promisee. That is to say, a party who has not furnished consideration may not bring an action to enforce a contract (*Dunlop Pneumatic Tyre Co v Selfridge* (1915, HL); *Tweddle v Atkinson* (1861)). As a general rule, where a contract is premised on the basis of an act followed by a promise, the consideration will be deemed to be 'past' consideration and will not be enforceable (*Roscorla v Thomas* (1842) (involving the sale of a horse); and *Re McArdle* (1951, CA) (involving household refurbishments). There are, however, a number of 'exceptions' to the rule that past consideration is not good consideration, the most important of which for present purposes is if there is an understanding that a good or service is to be paid for, albeit that no express agreement has been reached as to the amount payable before the time of performance— the 'requested performance exception' (see *Lampleigh v Braithwait* (1615), where the court held that there had been an implied promise to pay for the service rendered). There is also authority to suggest that the court may be more willing to imply a promise to pay when the issue involves a commercial arrangement rather than a domestic one. On this point see *Pao On v Lau Yiu Long* (1979, PC), where Lord Scarman laid down three requirements for this exception to operate:

- the act must have been at the promisor's request;
- the parties must have understood that the act was to be remunerated either by a payment or the conferment of some benefit; and
- the payment or benefit must have been legally enforceable had it been promised in advance.

(See also *Re Casey's Patents* (1892); and contrast *Re McArdle* which involved a domestic arrangement—though, in any case, the work had not been requested.)

It might seem, therefore, that since the act of fitting the lock has already been completed when J promises to pay S £50, J's promise is not enforceable (it has not been supported by consideration). However, applying the test laid down in *Pao On*, S would argue that (i) the promisor (J) requested that the act be performed, (ii) there was an implicit understanding that remuneration of some sort would be made for fitting the lock, and (iii) had the promise been made in advance, it would have been legally enforceable. In reply J might argue that this was merely a domestic arrangement (falling within *Balfour*) and not a commercial arrangement: it was a social agreement over coffee, to which legal relations were not to be attached—it was implicit that S was fitting the lock as a favour. The decision is finely balanced, but given S's state of penury—he was out of work and hard hit by the recession—of which J was probably aware, it seems reasonable to assume that this was a commercial arrangement where payment was implicit. On this basis, J's promise is legally enforceable.

Issue III: Does Simon have a good claim on the payment of £250 by Nicky?

Assuming that the initial agreement between S and N is not enforceable the issue arises whether the subsequent agreement is legally binding. S offers to finish the wall (which on this reading he is under no obligation to do) and in return N promises to pay him £250 to do so. S's consideration is the employment he forgoes/work he does, while N's consideration is her promise to pay S £250 on completion of the wall. There is clearly an intention to create legal relations, since S has turned down the opportunity to take on new work and explicitly says he needs payment (£250). Accordingly, N will be under a binding obligation to pay S the money owed.

If, however, the initial agreement between S and N amounts to a contract, then the issues are much more complex, involving the law applicable to variations of contracts and possibly the law on economic duress.

According to the rule in *Stilk v Myrick* (1809), the performance of an existing contractual duty as consideration for a further promise from the party to whom the existing duty was owed is not good consideration. Thus, in that case the promise of extra pay was held to be unenforceable (contrast *Hartley v Ponsonby*—where, in more extreme circumstances, the crew was deemed to have gone beyond its duty, and the extra payment promised was enforceable). In applying the rule in *Stilk*, it would seem that S has provided no fresh consideration for N's promise to pay him £250. Given that S has not gone beyond his duty, the more liberal rule in *Hartley v Ponsonby* does not apply. However, the principle in *Stilk* has been 'refined' in the Court of Appeal decision of *Williams v Roffey* (1990) where it was held that in the event of a further promise being made in a commercial context where both parties intended the further promise made to have legal force, consideration for that promise could be found in the 'practical benefit' conferred on the promisor (provided the promise was made because of this perceived benefit).

S could argue that, in accordance with the decision in *Williams*, the agreement between him and N was a commercial agreement, that both parties intended the further promises made to have legal force and that N does receive a practical benefit (e.g. getting the wall finished sooner rather than later) and it is this which induces her to make the additional promise. However, there are considerable difficulties in applying the principle in *Williams* to this situation. For example, there is no indication that N gains any factual benefit from the prompt completion of the wall. Moreover, there is a possibility that N's promise was not freely given, but was the result of illegitimate commercial pressure: *CTN* (1994, CA *per* Lord Steyn); *Huyton* (1999). Here, S 'tells' N that he cannot complete the wall unless she pays him the extra money. In *Williams*, the plaintiff fully intended to complete. Although the fact that N does not protest about the payment at the time, would help her claim that the additional promise was not freely given (*The Atlantic Baron* (1979)), it would nevertheless seem sensible to suggest that *Williams* is unlikely to prove helpful to S's claim for recovery of the £250.

It is worth noting that promissory estoppel as traditionally understood will not help S either. Although he relied to his detriment on N's promise, he could only use estoppel as a defence to a claim by N, and not as a cause of action to recover the money promised (*Combe v Combe* (1951, CA)).

In conclusion, S's best hope is that the initial agreement between him and N is not a contract, but that the later agreement concerning the £250 is. With respect to J, S appears to be on firmer ground since it seems likely that the court will hold that payment for the work was implicit.

Analysis

(a) Again it must be stressed that this method of carving the answer up into various questions, is not the only (or even best) way of answering this or, indeed, any other problem question—not least because it is always a good idea to demonstrate to the examiner that your mind is sufficiently flexible so as not to be wedded to one particular technique. Nevertheless, this type of approach is extremely effective. The right type of questions are asked and this helps 'set up' the answer, thus leaving the student with the task of filling in the boxes by writing out the relevant law and applying it to the facts.

(b) Note the different points raised by this type of contract formation question—in particular, whether there was:

- an agreement (which can be evidenced by an offer and an acceptance);
- an intention to create legal relations; and
- a promise supported by consideration.

In particular, note how the examiner leans towards the latter two issues, with different sub-issues being wrapped up inside them, e.g. consideration (past consideration and exceptions). This is extremely common and you must learn to move from the broader picture to those areas where detailed analysis is required.

(c) An alternative, and, perhaps slightly more sophisticated, approach which would have been equally good in relation to Issue II is as follows:

> At first sight it might appear that the agreement is not supported by consideration—the act of fitting the lock had already been completed when J promised to pay S £50—and the rule is that past consideration is not good consideration (see, e.g., *Re McArdle* (1951, CA)). However, there are a number of cases which provide evidence of at least one exception to this rule. In *Re Casey's Patents* (1892), it was held that the promise to pay a manager for services which had been undertaken prior to the promise *was* supported by consideration. Since payment was implicit, it was only the amount that needed to be settled. A similar result was reached in the case of *Lampleigh v Braithwait*. In the problem before us, the court might find that remuneration was expected, leaving only the amount to be settled. Since it is more likely that a promise to pay will be implied where there is a commercial arrangement rather than a domestic one (see *Pao On v Lau Yiu Long* (1979, PC)), it is possible that here S could persuade the court that this was more than a domestic arrangement (his need for work would be one argument in his favour). S would argue in accordance with Lord Scarman's test in *Pao On* that the act (fitting the lock) was done at the promisor's request (here, J), there was an implicit understanding that remuneration of some sort would be made for fitting the lock (he is already 'at work' when J approaches him), and had the promise been made in advance, it would have been legally enforceable. Although, by no means a foregone conclusion, S's argument is likely to win the day.

This is a more direct approach than the one used in the fuller answer above. One could discuss the reasons why one approach is better than the other, but the point is that both ways of presenting the material are along the right lines. In each passage, the issue is identified (consideration, in particular past consideration), the law is set out and it is applied to the facts. There is, however, a slight danger with this more direct approach. In particular, it encourages students to reach an early conclusion on a matter (which may, indeed be correct). However, by concluding too early, this could mean that you fail adequately to 'unpack' your material, resulting in a loss of marks.

Clearly, how you decide Issue I will influence your answer to Issue III. If the initial agreement between Simon and Nicky is not enforceable, then Issue III involves assessing the relatively straightforward matter of determining whether a contract is formed as a result of their later negotiations. If, however, there is an initial contract, you must discuss the law relating to modification of contracts. This is called 'arguing in the alternative' and a good answer is one which allows these options to be explored. Your conclusion on Issue I should therefore be provisional rather than definitive.

(d) Although the *Williams v Roffey* point in Issue III is difficult, it should not be ignored. The important thing for exam purposes is not to come up with the 'right' answer, but rather to make sure that your claims are supported by credible arguments. The aim is to recognize and comment upon difficulties rather than to gloss over them.

(e) In relation to promissory estoppel the answer claims:

> It is worth noting that promissory estoppel as traditionally understood will not help S either. Although S relied to his detriment on N's promise, he could only use estoppel as a defence to a claim by N, and not as a cause of action to recover the money promised (*Combe v Combe* (1951, CA)).

Strictly speaking this is correct—it represents the orthodox view of promissory estoppel as a 'shield' and not a 'sword'. However, it would not be inappropriate (and perhaps even desirable) to suggest that a different view might be taken if the issue were to be raised on appeal to the Court of Appeal or, in particular, the House of Lords. After all, proprietary estoppel gives rise to a cause of action, and as Scarman LJ remarked in *Crabb v Arun District Council* [1976] Ch 179, the distinction between promissory and proprietary estoppel was not one that he found convincing (implying therefore that promissory estoppel should also be a cause of action). Furthermore, there is academic opinion which is critical of the Court of Appeal's reasoning in *Combe v Combe* and which opens the door to the possibility of estoppel as a cause of action (see Atiyah, 'Consideration: A Restatement' in Atiyah (ed), *Essays on Contract* (1986, Oxford, Clarendon Press) 179). Finally, there is the ruling in *Walton Stores (Interstate) Ltd v Maher* (1988) 164 CLR 387. Although this is a decision of the Australian High Court, and is thus not binding in English law, it is nevertheless highly persuasive.

(f) There are two further aspects of the answer that are worthy of comment. First, the student seeks to 'lead' the discussion, not so much with cases, but with propositions of law, which are then supported by authority. For example:

> [C]onsideration must be sufficient (i.e. it must have some value in the eyes of the law), though it need not be adequate (*Chappell v Nestle* (1960, HL)). The consideration must also have moved

from the promisee. That is to say, a party who has not furnished consideration may not bring an action to enforce a contract (*Dunlop Pneumatic Tyre Co v Selfridge* (1915, HL); *Tweddle v Atkinson* (1861)). As a general rule, where a contract is premised on the basis of an act followed by a promise, the consideration will be deemed to be 'past' consideration and will not be enforceable (*Roscorla v Thomas* (1842) (involving the sale of a horse); and *Re McArdle* (1951, CA) (involving household refurbishments)).

Secondly, note how the ruling in *Hartely v Ponsonby* is contrasted with the rule in *Stilk v Myrick*:

> According to the rule in *Stilk v Myrick* (1809), the performance of an existing contractual duty as consideration for a further promise from the party to whom the existing duty was owed is not good consideration. Thus, in that case the promise of extra pay was held to be unenforceable (contrast *Hartley v Ponsonby*—where, in more extreme circumstances, the crew was deemed to have gone beyond its duty, and the extra payment promised was enforceable).

A discussion of *Hartley v Ponsonby* is not strictly necessary here, but its incidental mention indicates that the student recognizes this. Remember, the question exists as a 'hanger' for you to present your knowledge of the area of contract law which the question has been designed to test. In this respect, answering problem questions resembles a 'game', one rule of which is that you have *some* degree of latitude in the material that you may introduce.

(g) Finally, much has been made of IRAC as a method of tackling problem questions. The inspiration for approaching problem questions in this manner is derived from what judges do when writing their judgments. Below, we set out a passage from Lord Denning in *Oscar Chess Ltd v Williams* [1957] 1 WLR 370 (involving the sale of a second-hand car to a firm of dealers) which can be characterized in IRAC terms:

> **[Issue]**   The crucial question is: was it a binding promise [here, a warranty] or only an innocent misrepresentation? **[The significance lies in the type of remedy that is available]** . . .
>
> **[Rule(s)]**   It is instructive to take some [examples] to show how the courts have approached this question. When the seller states a fact which is or should be within his own knowledge and of which the buyer is ignorant, intending that the buyer should act on it, and he does so, it is easy to infer a warranty: see *Couchman v Hill* [1951, CA], where the farmer stated that the heifer was unserved, and *Harling v Eddy* [1947, CA] where he stated that there was nothing wrong with her. So also if he makes a promise about something which is or should be within his own control: see *Birch v Paramount Estates Ltd* [1956, CA], where the seller stated that the house would be as good as the show house. But if the seller, when he states a fact, makes it clear that he has no knowledge of his own but has got his information elsewhere and is merely passing it on, it is not so easy to imply a warranty. Such a case was *Routledge v McKay* [1954] where the seller 'stated that it was a 1942 model and pointed to the corroboration found in the book', and it was held that there was no warranty.
>
> **[Apply]**   Turning now to the present case, much depends on . . .

Note, in particular, how adroitly Lord Denning marshalls the relevant legal propositions (all the while alluding to the key facts of each of the cases cited).

2 Exemption clauses

In an exemption clause question the focus of the answer is not on whether a contract has been formed. Rather, the focus is on the obligations owed by the parties under the contract. That is to say, your primary aim in answering such a question should be on addressing the nature and extent of the rights and obligations which arise under the contract rather than establishing whether the contract has come into existence in the first place. Unlike the rather 'bitty' nature of questions on formation, there is more of a definite framework available for exemption/limitation clause questions around which to weave your material. This should become clear by reading the answer to the following question.

Question

Fry, who was on his way to a book sale, stopped at a fun fair on Bristol Downs, and decided to have a go on 'Laurie's Bumper Cars'. Laurie took his money, and Fry started to drive round. Laurie, however, who was still collecting money, slipped and fell on to the car in front, which stopped suddenly, causing Fry's car to crash into it. After the turmoil has subsided, Fry discovered that a valuable first edition of '*Jeeves and Wooster*', which he had been taking to the sale, had fallen out of his pocket and had been ruined by the bumper car running over it; and that he himself had suffered a whiplash injury. He asked Laurie, 'What are you going to do about it? It's all your fault.' Laurie replied by shrugging his shoulders and pointing to a large sign on the stand saying 'Patrons go on the bumpers at their own risk. No responsibility accepted for any injuries or damage.' These words were repeated on the back of the ticket which Fry had bought.
Advise Fry.

Suggested answer

It would appear that Laurie (L) is prima facie liable for damages for breach of contract, since it could be argued that under s 13 of the Sale of Goods and Services Act 1983, there has been a breach of the implied term that the supplier of a service (here, Bumper Cars), acting in the course of a business, must use reasonable care and skill. In order to escape liability, L would need to show that the exemption clause was legally valid. **[This last sentence neatly introduces the significance of the exemption clause.]**

The first issue in this respect is whether the exclusion clause was **incorporated** into the contract to use the bumper cars. **[This is an issue of incorporation.]** An exclusion clause may only become a term of the contract if reasonable notice of its existence is given before, or at the time when, the contract is made: *Olley v Marlborough Court* (1949, CA). From the facts of the question, incorporation of the relevant term is possible via two routes: (a) the ticket; and (b) the sign.

The Ticket: There is authority to support the proposition that a notice printed on a ticket (as in this problem) may be effective to exclude liability even though it is not actually delivered to the plaintiff until after the moment of agreement between the parties: *Parker v SE Railway* (1877, CA). However, in *Chapelton v Barry UDC* (1940, CA) the court refused to recognize a ticket as a contractual document at all, treating it merely as a receipt for money paid—notice of the clause came too late, since the offer and the acceptance preceded the issuing of the ticket. More recent authorities indicate that reasonable notice must be given and *Parker* may be better interpreted as a case where on the facts reasonable notice was provided. It is important to note, however, that *Parker* might not be decided in the same way today. In *Thornton v Shoe Lane Parking Ltd* (1971, CA), for example, Lord Denning thought that for sufficient notice to be given in a 'ticket' case, it would need to be clearly drawn to the plaintiff's attention (see also *Interfoto Picture Library v Stiletto Visual Programmes* (1988, CA), where it was held that if the clause is particularly onerous or unusual then it may need to be more clearly drawn to the other party's attention). Whether reasonable steps have been taken to bring the clause to the attention of Fry is a question of fact. Since the decision in *Parker* should be treated with caution, it seems highly unlikely that sufficient notice has been given for the exclusion clause printed on the ticket to be effective.

The Sign: Whether the sign is incorporated into the contract must also be viewed in the light of the rule mentioned in *Olley* (above). In that case the exclusion clause was read by a hotel guest in the room after booking into the hotel. So reasonable notice had not been given. In the problem before us, however, we are told that L has erected a 'large sign' excluding liability. Thus, in the absence of other facts (e.g. that the sign was hidden from view), it can be argued that F did have reasonable notice of the sign—and thus of the legal obligations which L was prepared to undertake. On this basis the exclusion clause would be incorporated.

Assuming that the exclusion clause does become a term of the contract, L may only rely upon it to escape liability if the wording of the clause specifically covers the type of liability in question (i.e. the loss or damage which has arisen). **[This is a matter of construction or interpretation.]** The courts will not imply an exemption greater than that contained in the words used. For example, in *Houghton v Trafalgar Insurance* (1954) a clause which excluded liability when a car was carrying a *load* in excess of that for which it was constructed, did not exclude liability where the car was carrying an excessive number of *passengers* (see also *Andrews v Singer* (1934, CA)). Where the words in the clause are ambiguous, the courts construe them *contra proferentem*, that is, against the person seeking to rely on them. Thus, in *White v John Warwick* (1953), the Court of Appeal construed an exclusion clause similar to the one in issue in the question as being sufficient to exclude strict contractual liability for personal injury, but not sufficient to exclude liability for injury caused negligently (see also *Hollier v Rambler Motors*, 1972, CA). Very clear words indeed are required to exclude liability in negligence.

On the facts, there is the possibility of strict contractual liability for breach of an implied term that the obligation contracted for (a bumper car ride) would actually be achieved. Laurie could argue that, properly construed, the exclusion clause covers this—an argument which is probably correct. However, the contract is one of providing a 'service' and therefore falls within s 13, Supply of Goods and Services Act 1982, which implies a term into such a contract that the service will be carried out with reasonable care and skill (i.e. not negligently). The contract has not been so carried out, since Laurie has been negligent—it was foreseeable that an accident might happen if he continued to collect money after the cars had started. There has, therefore, been a negligent breach of contract. Applying *White* (above), the exclusion clause will probably not be sufficient to cover liability under s 13.

If, however, this argument is incorrect and the clause properly construed does cover the breach, there is still a possibility that an exclusion clause may be rendered ineffective by virtue of either the **Unfair Terms in Consumer Contracts Regulations 1999** or by the **Unfair Contract Terms Act 1977** (UCTA). **[This involves an assessment of whether the clause offends 'legislative' provisions.]**

The Regulations apply to 'any term in a contract concluded between a seller or supplier and a consumer where the ... term has not been individually negotiated' (reg 5). A 'seller' is a person who sells goods or who in entering into contracts does so for purposes relating to his business (reg 3); a 'supplier' is a person who supplies goods or services and in making contracts does so for purposes relating to his business (reg 3). A 'consumer' means a natural person, who acts for purposes which are outside his business (reg 3). Prima facie, the contract between F and L falls within the Regulations because it is a standard form contract (it has not been individually negotiated), Laurie is offering services (a bumper car ride) in the course of business, and Fry has entered into the contract for reasons of pleasure not business.

The effect of the Regulations is to render *unfair terms* inoperative. These are defined as 'any term[s] which, contrary to the requirement of good faith, [cause] a significant imbalance in the parties' rights and obligations arising under the contract, to the detriment of the consumer' (reg 5). Factors taken into account in determining good faith include: the nature of the goods or services; the bargaining position of the parties; whether the seller has dealt fairly and equitably with the consumer; and any other relevant factors. Where there is doubt about the meaning of a written term, the interpretation most favourable to the consumer will prevail. Where the term is held to be 'unfair', it will not be binding on the consumer. The Regulations give an indicative list of terms which are prima facie considered to breach the requirement of good faith, one of which is a term which purports to exclude/limit liability for death or personal injury. Although this is not conclusive, it seems likely that the exclusion clause will be inoperative insofar as F seeks to recover damages for the physical injury (whiplash) that he has sustained (see: Sch 3, para 1(a)). But even if the Regulations are held not to apply, s 2(1) UCTA places an absolute prohibition on terms which purport to exclude liability for death or personal injury resulting from negligence in contracts between a supplier acting in the course of a business and a consumer, as in this case.

Damage to F's property (the book) is somewhat more problematic. Under the Regulations, terms which exclude liability other than for death or personal injury are prima facie unfair only if the exclusion is 'inappropriate' (Sch 3, para 1(b)). In this case, therefore, F may have to rely on s 2(2), UCTA 1977. The effect of the exclusion clause is determined on the basis of whether the term is a fair and reasonable one to have been included in the light of the circumstances known (or which ought to have been) to the parties at the time the contract is made (s 11). The burden of showing that the clause is 'reasonable' is on the person so claiming (here, L): s 11(5). It seems reasonable for a user of bumper cars to assume that the owner would not act negligently or seek to exclude liability for anything which was within the owner's control. F would therefore be entitled to recover damages for his injuries and for the value of the book.

Analysis

(a) The words in bold (incorporation, construction, legislative provisions represent the key areas on which much of your reading about this topic will have been based. Not surprisingly, it is upon these 'pegs' that the answer has been hung. These issues provide the framework/structure for the answer. Whatever the approach adopted, these issues would have to be confronted in some sort of logical format. Note, that in this instance, the answer starts with a conclusion and then justifies this conclusion *by way of reasoned argument*.

(b) Note also, that the issue of the ticket as an exclusion clause is considered first and then rejected before going on to consider the legal significance of the sign (which is deemed to be incorporated). If you were to do it the other way round, you would incorporate the sign, thus making the issue of whether the ticket is an exclusion clause redundant. As you are an examinee, your overall aim ought to be to display as much *relevant* knowledge to the examiner as possible, even if this may seem highly artificial at times.

(c) In discussing the Regulations most of the relevant law is set out first (the definition of the terms) and then applied. During the 'application' stage, an additional legal rule is introduced, namely:

> The Regulations give an indicative list of terms which are prima facie considered to breach the requirement of good faith, one of which is a term that purports to exclude/limit liability for death or personal injury.

Keeping material like this 'in reserve' is a perfectly sensible approach to use and is illustrative of the fact that any approach adopted must be sufficiently flexible to accommodate slightly different ways of analysing problems. In contrast to the approach used in discussing the Regulations, the material in relation to UCTA 1977 is handled more sparingly. The law is not set out first and then applied; rather, fact and law are intertwined.

3   Misrepresentation and (some) mistake

The existence of 'vitiating factors', such as misrepresentation and mistake, can affect the validity of a contract that parties have entered into. The answers to the remaining questions in this chapter illustrate this issue well. Note how the 'scheme' presented below can be used as a way of helping you to *think* about, and subsequently structure, your answer:

- Are the statements representations or terms?
- If they are representations, are they actionable (i.e. are they misrepresentations which induce the other party to enter into the contract)?
- If they are misrepresentations, of what type are they (i.e., fraudulent, negligent, or wholly innocent)?
- What remedies are available?

As we have already seen, when considering how you will tackle an exam question (or, indeed, any legal problem), it may be helpful to ask yourself: what exactly does the party seeking advice want—damages?, rescission?, the return of the property from an innocent third party?, and so on. Thinking along these lines will enable you to identify legal doctrines which may help you to achieve what it is that your client wants (albeit that there are, no doubt, a number of hurdles that need to be negotiated before the particular result is achieved).

Question

(i) Gerard, who has won a large sum of money, goes to Rod, who owns an exclusive art gallery in London. Gerard points at a painting and says 'Tell me about this one. How much are you asking?' Rod, who knows that the painting is by a minor English artist, says, 'I cannot be absolutely certain, but it is my opinion that it is a Renoir. I'll sell it to you for £100,000.' Gerard buys the painting, which is actually worth only £5,000.

AND

(ii) David, a wealthy art collector, visits Rod and they enthuse together about a painting hanging in the gallery. 'It's a beautiful example of Botticelli's work,' says Rod. David, who normally only collects English landscapes, buys the painting for £100,000 as a present for his girlfriend, and arranges to take the painting away. Unfortunately the painting is damaged in transit, and when David takes it to a restorer, he is told that the painting is actually by a pupil of Botticelli, and would really be worth only £20,000, after restoration, which would cost £6,000. In fact there had recently been an article about the painting in an art journal, to which both David and Rod subscribe, reattributing the work.

What remedies, if any, do Gerard and David have against Rod?

Suggested answer

(i) Gerard and Rod

Gerard (G) will want to sue Rod (R) for damages and/or he may want to rescind the contract (i.e. have it set aside). Applying an objective test of the parties' intentions, the statement made by R is probably a representation rather than a term—(*Schawel v Reade*, 1913, HL). If this is correct, the issue then arises as to whether the representation is actionable—whether R made a *false statement of fact*, which, whilst not a term of the contract, *induced G* to enter the contract. A 'mere puff' (*Carlill v Carbolic Smoke Ball*, 1893, CA) will not amount to a misrepresentation; neither will a statement of opinion (*Bisset v Wilkinson*, 1927, PC). However, where the opinion offered is dishonest, the false statement can amount to a misrepresentation (*Smith v Land & House Property Corp* (1884)). Given that R 'knows' the painting is not a Renoir, but says that it is, he has 'knowingly' made a 'false statement of fact' (the fact of whether or not that is his honest opinion). In this respect, the qualification 'I cannot be absolutely certain . . .', when taken in its context, is irrelevant.

The next issue to consider is whether the false statement of fact *induces* G to enter into the contract. Usually, this means that G must show that the statement was material (i.e. that it would cause a reasonable person considering entering into the contract to decide positively in favour of doing so). However, where there is fraud (as here) this requirement is dispensed with (*Smith v Kay* (1859)). It would seem that all that must be shown is that G relied on R's statement (contrast *Attwood v Small* (1838), where P relied on an independent expert's advice and so was denied a remedy for misrepresentation). The fact that G was given the opportunity to test its accuracy is irrelevant (*Redgrave v Hurd* (1881, CA)), as is the fact that R's misrepresentation may not be the only reason why G entered into the contract: *Edgington v Fitzmaurice* (1885).

The next issue is to decide what type of misrepresentation has been made: fraudulent, negligent, or innocent? This is important from the point of view of the remedies granted by the courts. On the facts of the problem, the misrepresentation is fraudulent, since R has knowingly made a false statement (*Derry v Peek* (1889, HL)). Damages are available and are calculated on tortious (out-of-pocket) principles, rather than contractual (loss-of-bargain) principles (fraudulent misrepresentation is the tort of deceit).

[*   *   *   *]

In addition to damages, a fraudulent misrepresentation renders the contract voidable. In other words, G could get an order for rescission. Where the contract is rescinded, the object is to put the parties back in the position they would have been in had the contract never been made. However, certain 'bars' to rescission exist (i.e. in certain circumstances P may lose his right to rescind). The most important 'bar' from G's point of view is where P is deemed to have *affirmed* the contract. Lapse of time may be evidence of affirmation: *Leaf v International Galleries* (1950, CA).

[*   *   *   *]

(ii) David and Rod

Applying the test set out in part (i), it would appear that R's statement, 'It's a beautiful example of Botticelli's work' is, again, a false statement of fact. However, it is less certain whether there has been an inducement. If David (D) buys the painting irrespective of whether it is by Botticelli, but simply because he knows his girlfriend will like it, then no inducement will have occurred, since he has not relied on R's statement (*Attwood v Small*). On the other hand, if his girlfriend likes only Botticelli, this will be strong evidence that R's statement was a material factor in inducing D to enter into the contract. Alternatively, even if his girlfriend does like only Botticelli it could be inferred that since D subscribes to the art journal he relies only on his own judgement and not R's. However, his failure to inform R of this matter (i.e. to put him right) is surely significant, since it implies that he was not aware of the reattribution (though, equally, this may raise an issue of contributory negligence on D's part).

On the assumption that an inducement exists, it is again necessary to classify the misrepresentation and so determine the remedies available. In this instance there is no indication of the type of misrepresentation made. If it is fraudulent, the above mentioned rules in part (i) will apply. If the misrepresentation is negligent (i.e. it is a statement that no reasonable man would have made), then remedies are available at common law and under statute. At common law, damages are available in certain circumstances for the tort of negligent misstatement (*Hedley Byrne*, 1964, HL). More relevant to the present problem, however, is s 2(1) of the Misrepresentation Act 1967 which has significant advantages over a claim at common law. This section assumes that all non-fraudulent statements are negligent and shifts the burden on the maker of the statement to disprove negligence. However, the alleged misrepresentor will not have to pay damages if he proves that:

(a) he had reasonable grounds to believe; *and*

(b) did believe up to the time the contract was made that the facts represented were true.

As the alleged misrepresentor, R could argue that he had not read the journal and thus reasonably believed that what he was saying was true, and that this is what he did believe until after the contract was formed. Notwithstanding this, D is in a very strong position, since the burden of proof is on R. Therefore, it would seem likely that D would be entitled to damages. According to the Court of Appeal in *Royscot v Rogerson* (1991), these are calculated on the same basis as fraudulent misrepresentation (i.e. all consequential losses, even if those losses are not reasonably foreseeable—compare the position under *Hedley Byrne* where damages are calculated on what was reasonably foreseeable). Again, D will be entitled to rescind the contract, subject to any bars.

It is also possible that the misrepresentation was innocent (i.e. a statement made by a person who *has* reasonable grounds for believing in its truth, but which is nonetheless false). If a misrepresentation is wholly innocent then the victim is only entitled to rescission (and an indemnity, see below). However, according to s 2(2), Misrepresentation Act 1967 the court has a discretion, where the other party would be entitled to rescind, to award damages instead of rescission—and perhaps even where the misrepresentation in question is not sufficient to ground a right of rescission: *William Sindall v Cambridgeshire CC* (1994, CA). Where rescission is available, it is generally possible to recover an indemnity as well. An indemnity provides compensation for expenditure incurred as a result of obligations which have been created by the contract into which the representee has been induced to enter (see *Whittington v Seale-Hayne* (1900)).

Although the painting has been damaged in transit, and it might seem that this creates a bar to rescission, it is not necessary for there to be exact restoration; the remedy is still available if substantial restoration is possible. Although the exact nature of the damage done is not specified, it would seem that substantial restoration is possible and that the court could therefore use its discretion to award damages in lieu of rescission.

D could also allege that the contract is void for mistake (here, common mistake—the parties, though in apparent agreement, have contracted on the same false assumption). Although it is possible that a contract will make provision for allocation of risk in the event of some shared misunderstanding, there is no evidence to suppose that this rule is relevant here. The common law admittedly takes a very narrow view of the type of mistake which will render a contract void for common mistake (and thus for it to be deemed never to have existed): it must be shown that there was a shared fundamental mistake as to the *existence* of the subject matter of the contract (*Bell v Lever* (1931, HL)). However three of their Lordships in *Bell* did say that a sufficiently fundamental mistake as to quality might render the contract void at common law. This was especially so where the mistake rendered the thing 'essentially different' from that which it was believed to be. Nevertheless, in applying this test, their Lordships took such a restrictive view that it has been doubted whether any mistake as to quality can ever be sufficiently fundamental at common law as to render the contract void. On this reading of *Bell*, it would seem highly unlikely that the mistake as to quality in the problem (mistaking the pupil for the master) would be legally operative (see also *Leaf*, a case on similar facts to the problem). However, it has been suggested that *Bell* is a 'quite exceptional case' (*Associated Japanese Bank v Credit Nord* (1988) *per* Steyn J) and there are those who would say that a better (though not generally accepted) view is that such a mistake should be regarded as sufficiently fundamental to render the contract void (*Treitel*).

The Court of Appeal's recent ruling in *The Great Peace* would seem to preclude an equitable remedy (overruling *Solle v Butcher* (1950, CA)).

Analysis

(a) The first point to note relates to the identification of the legal issues. As suggested earlier, the legal significance of the various statements made are analysed in relation to the relevant legal rules. For example, in part (i), the statement 'I cannot be absolutely certain, but it is my opinion that it is a Renoir' is analysed in terms of its legal significance: is it a term or merely a representation; and, if it is the latter, is it actionable?

(b) The second point relates to structure: you will see that the organizing framework revolves around pairing up the parties. Within this framework, there has been adopted in part (i) a variation of the IRAC method. If you were to adopt this modified version of IRAC you would need to:

- identify the relevant remedies appropriate to the parties (here, damages and rescission);
- state the law relating to the remedy sought—the cause of action (the law on misrepresentation); and
- apply the law to the facts, stating what further facts (if any) you would need to provide more concrete advice.

This approach is not, however, without its difficulties. Most significantly, it requires a student at the outset of the answer to make an accurate assessment of the relevant remedies available and the steps that must be covered in order to secure those remedies. This may be asking a lot of a student, especially in the 'heat' of an exam. However, that said, students usually decide early on in the assessment of the question where the balance of liability lies, and thus do have a rough idea of where the answer will end up. This ability to survey the terrain quickly and find out the 'lie of the land' is invaluable in determining the relevant remedies.

(c) The third point to note relates to the application of the relevant law to the facts. In both parts (i) and (ii), the law on misrepresentation is set out in stages and applied. For example:

- the false statement;
- the inducement; and
- the remedies; and so on.

Setting out the law in stages like this helps you to formulate your answer, and helps the examiner to follow what you are doing and where you are going. In part (ii), although there is clearly a false statement, it is a lot less certain whether an inducement has occurred. But to prevent an early 'exit' from the question the conclusion is made that an inducement does exist. For example:

> However, it is less certain whether there has been an inducement. If D buys the painting irrespective of whether it is by Botticelli, but simply because he knows his girlfriend will like it, then no inducement will have occurred, since he has not relied on R's statement (*Attwood v Small*). On the other hand, if his girlfriend likes only Botticelli, this will be strong evidence that R's statement was a material factor in inducing D to enter into the contract. Alternatively, even if his girlfriend does like only Botticelli it could be inferred that since D subscribes to the art journal he relies only on his own judgment and not R's. However, his failure to inform R of this matter (i.e. to put him right) is surely significant, since it implies that he was not aware of the reattribution (though, equally, this may raise an issue of contributory negligence on D's part).
> On the assumption that an inducement exist . . .

This sort of approach is permissible only if you have canvassed arguments for both points of view and there are at least some plausible arguments in favour of your conclusion, albeit that the matter is a finely balanced one.

(d) It will no doubt have struck you that the answer is very long; and if—as in this answer—you have a lot of ground to cover, you may need to modify the way in which you set out the law and apply it to the facts. This will mean that instead of explaining the law and then applying it to the facts, you have to interweave law and fact more adroitly. This sort of approach is more sophisticated, since it is much less formulaic. The down side, however, is that it is harder to teach to students, since the processes involved are altogether more subtle and if not done properly could result in the loss of marks. A good example of the approach in action is as follows:

> Given that R has knowingly made a false statement of fact, the misrepresentation is fraudulent (*Derry v Peek* (1889, HL)) and damages are payable on the basis of tortious (out-of-pocket) principles.

Yet again:

> Since there is an argument that a bar to rescission exists (the painting has been 'damaged in transit'—so restoration is no longer possible) it might seem that the court will be unable to exercise its discretion to award damages in lieu of rescission in accordance with s 2(2), Misrepresentation Act 1967. However, in the light of the Court of Appeal's decision in *William Sindall v Cambridgeshire CC* (1994), it may no longer be necessary for rescission to be available before this remedy can be granted.

Be careful with such an approach since, as was mentioned earlier, students have a tendency to gloss over their reasoning when reaching conclusions. Be sure to 'unpack' all the material which has led you to reach the conclusion(s) you have.

4 Mistake and (some) misrepresentation

Question

Margaret, a direct descendant of Charles Dickens, owns a valuable portrait of that author. Advise Margaret in both the following alternative situations.

(i) Dick, who falsely claims to be Sir Raymond Brotherby, the famous art dealer, offers her £10,000 for the painting. She agrees to sell for this price, but when Dick says he would like to pay by cheque, she says the deal is off. She is persuaded to part with the painting after telephoning Sir Raymond's office in London, at Dick's suggestion. Sir Raymond's secretary confirms that Sir Raymond is bald and has a ginger moustache, a description that also applies to Dick. Dick subsequently sells the painting to Hilary and disappears. The cheque is dishonoured.

(ii) Margaret is reluctant to sell the painting at all, since it is a family heirloom. However, she is persuaded to do so by Dick, who this time falsely claims to be the curator of the National Portrait Gallery. He says that the painting will have a good home and will be available to a wide audience, convincing Margaret that selling the painting would be a public-spirited thing to do. He produces a bogus identity card and pays by cheque, which is dishonoured. He sells the painting to Richard and then disappears.

Suggested answer

Part (i)

Although Margaret (M) undoubtedly has a claim for fraudulent misrepresentation, in view of the fact that Dick (D) has disappeared she will not be able successfully to recover damages from him. Similarly, assuming Hilary (H) is a bona fide purchaser for value, M will be unable to claim the equitable remedy of rescission, since the property has already passed to H. Consequently, M's best option is to seek to have the contract with D declared void for unilateral mistake. **[Note how hopeless claims have been 'killed off'.]** A unilateral mistake encompasses the situation where one of the parties (here M) is mistaken and the other party (here, D) is aware of the mistake. Under a void contract, property cannot pass and M will be able to reclaim the property from H, irrespective of whether D's cheque has been dishonoured or whether D has disappeared.

Notwithstanding the recent ruling by the House of Lords in *Shogun Finance v Hudson* (2004), the law on unilateral mistake remains in a somewhat confused state—at least in relation to face-to-face transactions. The principle to be derived from the leading cases of *King's Norton* and *Cundy v Lindsay* is that if P considers the other party's identity to be important then the contract will be rendered void. If, on the other hand, P's mistake is merely regarding attributes (e.g., the social position, creditworthiness, etc. of the party with whom the contract is formed) it will not render the contract void. This distinction is illustrated by the facts of both *King's Norton* and *Cundy* v *Lindsay*. **[Discuss the facts of these cases. However, avoid simply reciting the facts. Instead show how the facts *illustrate* the point you are trying to make.]**

It could, however, be argued that this 'identity/attributes' approach involves a distinction without a difference. According to Lord Denning in *Lewis v Avery*, people are identified by reference to their attributes. What is more, it is a particularly difficult distinction to draw, especially when the parties deal, not by letter (as in *King's Norton* and *Cundy*), but face-to-face (see *Phillips v Brooks* (1919, CA); *Ingram v Little* (1960, CA); and *Lewis v Averay* (1971, CA)). The normal presumption when dealing face-to-face is that there is an intention to deal with the person who is physically present (*per* Pearce LJ in *Ingram v Little*). **[Again, you could profitably discuss the facts of some of these cases.]** However, this presumption is capable of being rebutted where the identity of the other party is of 'vital importance'. The House of Lords' decision in *Shogun Finance* (where the majority decided that the transaction at issue was 'by correspondence' and not 'face-to-face') is, sadly, of little help.

Applying the above principles to the facts . . . **[On the one hand, it could be argued that by telephoning Sir Raymond's office M is not merely seeking to verify the reliability of the cheque, but *rather* she is seeking to authenticate Dick's claim to be Sir Raymond—he has the same looks (bald and ginger). On the other hand, it could be said that (in line with the normal legal presumption outlined in *Ingram v Little*) M intended to contract with the person before her. That is to say, M's concerns went merely to the other party's creditworthiness. After all, she agrees to the price of £10,000—it is the manner of payment that is her concern. The latter is probably the better view—certainly it is the more orthodox.]**

Part (ii)

Again, while there is a prima facie case of fraudulent misrepresentation, this is unlikely to help M, since once more D has disappeared and there is no suggestion that Richard (R) is anything other than a bona fide purchaser for value, thus barring rescission. As in part (i), M's best option is to allege that the contract is void for unilateral mistake. In this instance, however, there is a stronger argument for saying that the contract is void because M was very interested in dealing with a particular person (i.e. her decision to contract is based on the person's identity rather than that person's creditworthiness). [**You could discuss some of the cases where the presumption that when the parties deal face-to-face they intended to contract with one another has, in fact, been rebutted—e.g. *Hardman v Booth*, *Lake v Summer*, and *Ingram v Little*. D's claims as to his identity are of vital importance, since M, as a direct descendant of Dickens, cares that the family heirloom will be given a 'good home' and will be available to a 'wide audience'. Furthermore, M is convinced that selling the painting is a 'public-spirited' thing to do.]**

[**Note how the actual words of the question are used when it comes to applying the law to the facts.**]

Analysis

Again, note the approach that has been used. Here, the answer has located the relevant area of contract law: mistake (with a fleeting reference to fraudulent misrepresentation). The significance of a legally operative mistake is outlined (i.e. severe consequences—the contract is void). The type of mistake is identified (unilateral) and a definition is provided. The answer goes on to provide an example of such a mistake. Subsequently the relevant law is set out (i.e. when is a mistake legally operative?). Following this, it is applied to the facts.

5   Summary

- As we have seen, all exam questions are essentially about the rights and liabilities/ obligations/duties of the parties. You must begin *to think* in this way.

- Do not—as most students do—seek to explain the problem question in terms of its facts (e.g. 'X has done . . . and in turn a disgruntled Y has done that'). Rather, *identify legal issues in relation to specific facts* (e.g. 'the issue here is whether X may enforce Y's promise to have the work completed by Friday').

- Although the existence of a contract is central to all contract problem questions, it is not the *focus* of all contract questions. Consequently, you do not need to waste time on issues of formation if it is clear that a contract exists and no-one would care to dispute it. Those questions which require a *detailed* examination of 'offer and acceptance' issues are usually obvious from their fact patterns.

- Although it is essential that you cite relevant authorities for the propositions of law which you outline, don't worry that different tutors (and textbook writers) emphasize different cases—there is usually more than one authority that can be used in support of a proposition of law. Provided you cite a critical mass of relevant authorities, you will still score highly.

- Sometimes in handling your material it is better to interweave the relevant law with the facts of the question. This is a more direct approach than the standard

IRAC method. One could discuss the reasons why one approach is better than the other, but the point is that both ways of presenting your material are along the right lines.

- In the event that you do begin a section of your answer with a conclusion on an issue (e.g. X will be able to claim rescission of the contract between him and Y), make sure that you fully demonstrate the reasoning that has led you to your conclusion. Poorly supported conclusions (even if 'correct') will result in you losing marks.

- Although the law may be against your client, there is always the possibility of taking your case on appeal in the hope that a higher court will overturn contrary authority—this is more likely to occur if your case involves a controversial legal issue (e.g. *Combe v Combe*; *Foakes v Beer*; and *Royscot v Rogerson*).

- As always, the aim is not to produce the definitive answer to the question set, but instead to ensure that you cover—in a credible and confident fashion—as many of the key points which the tutor has decided to test in the question set.

- Learn to 'argue in the alternative' (e.g. 'X could argue that . . .; failing this, he could seek to claim that . . .').

- When discussing the facts of cases, avoid simply reciting the facts. Instead, show how the facts *illustrate* the point you are trying to make.

4 Public law

At first sight it might seem that public law (sometimes also known as constitutional and administrative law) is unsuited to the application of a common problem-solving approach. After all, the wide-ranging nature of public law—spanning criminal and civil liability and touching on *political* as well as legal sanctions—suggests that it is very different from the other subjects we have so far considered. In the absence of a codified British constitution students are often 'thrown' by the flexibility of the subject matter and, in particular, by the influence of politics in the area of constitutional law (e.g. the significance of constitutional conventions). However, a number of the difficulties and significant differences that do exist may be mitigated by the fact that, as a general rule, some areas of public law are less likely to be examined in problem form than others. For example, it is unusual (though nevertheless still possible) to see a problem question on areas such as the sources of the British Constitution, the rule of law, or constitutional conventions. The conceptual nature of these topics means that they tend to appear in examinations as essay questions (see Chapter 5). By contrast, other areas of public law (e.g. police powers, public order, public interest immunity, European Community law, and judicial review) can easily be examined in problem form.

Yet notwithstanding the fact that public law poses significant challenges for students, these are not of such a magnitude that they invalidate the methods employed in earlier sections of this book. Consequently, in public law problem questions you must continue to identify legal issues (albeit that they may also raise political issues); you must extract the relevant rules and principles of law; and you must apply these rules to factual scenarios in order to reach credible conclusions.

In this chapter, we discuss problem questions from each of the three parts into which most public law courses are divided:

- general principles of constitutional law;
- the rights and liberties of the individual; and
- administrative law.

Note, however, that your course may have a different emphasis and you should bear this in mind when considering the material presented below. On general principles of constitutional law, we look at two questions that raise issues relevant to Parliamentary Supremacy, European Community law, the Human Rights Act 1998, and judicial accountability. For the civil liberties section, a police powers/public order question is attempted. Lastly, administrative law is tackled by way of a problem question on judicial review. In addition to employing the more general techniques already outlined and adopted in earlier chapters, special attention is again paid to 'micro structures', which will be of help in answering questions in the above specified areas.

1 Constitutional law

Question

Ral is a British citizen. As a practising Phob (a long-established minority religious group), Ral is required by the tenets of his faith to cover his head at all times in public, by wearing a large soft woollen hat called a 'kap'. Ral works in the construction trade on a building site, where all workers are legally required to wear 'hard hats' (safety helmets). However, for the last decade, as a result of the EC Commission Regulation No 100/1996 (fictitious), Ral and other Phob workers have been specifically excluded from this requirement and have been allowed to wear their kaps at the workplace.

One morning Ral is called into the office of Bob, the site manager. Bob explains that the company has been forced to introduce a new policy and that, to comply with the recently enacted Protection of Workers Act 2006 (fictitious), all workers in the construction trade must now wear 'hard hats' on site. Bob explains that unless Ral removes his kap and replaces it with a company issued 'hard hat', his monthly contract of employment will not be renewed.

Ignoring any issues relating to religious/racial discrimination or employment law, advise Ral.

Suggested answer

Can Ral rely on the EC Regulation to enable him to continue wearing his kap?

[The answer begins by identifying a relevant legal issue on the facts.] In addressing the issue of whether an Act of Parliament (here, the Protection of Workers Act 2006) can take precedence over a piece of European Community legislation (here, Regulation No 100/1996), the position of the European Court of Justice (ECJ) is clear. **[The relevant law is then set out.]** In such instances EC law prevails over subsequent incompatible national law (*Internationale Handelsgesellschaft* (1970, ECJ)). Were this not the case, the attainment of Community objectives would be jeopardized (*Costa v ENEL* (1964, ECJ)). Thus, EC law has created a 'new order of international law' by which states have limited their sovereign rights in certain areas (*Van Gend en Loos* (1963, ECJ)). Since the ECJ has instructed national courts that they must 'disapply' national law which is in conflict with EC law, it is indisputable that from the perspective of the European Court of Justice, EC law is supreme.

Significantly, for Ral (R), British law has adopted the same approach. Despite the fact that the UK courts have long held that an Act of Parliament is not invalid if it conflicts with a treaty to which the UK is a signatory (*Cheney v Conn* (1968)), the Treaty of Rome and the other treaties establishing the EC are not ordinary treaties—they have been incorporated into British law by way of the European Communities Act (ECA) 1972. The primacy of Community law was accepted by the House of Lords in *R v Secretary of State for Transport, ex p Factortame (No 2)* (1991), where a group of Spanish fishermen complained that certain provisions of the Merchant Shipping Act 1988 prevented them from registering their boats in the UK. They sought an interim injunction, claiming that parts of the 1988 Act were incompatible with EC law prohibiting discrimination against other Community nationals. Following a preliminary ruling from the ECJ, the House of Lords ruled that it was the duty of a British court to override any rule of national law which was in direct conflict with a directly enforceable rule of EC law.

[The above law is applied and a conclusion is then reached.] In view of the fact that regulations are 'directly applicable' and do not require Member States to take any action for them to become part of their national law (EC Treaty, Art 249), Regulation No 100/1996 will take precedence over the Act in this scenario (*Factortame*). The House of Lords has subsequently approved the *Factortame* decision (*R v Employment Secretary, ex p EOC* (1995, HL)), so Ral's argument that EC law should prevail over the 2006 Act is likely to be successful.

Ral's remedies under the Human Rights Act 1998

Ral is also likely to argue that the Act of Parliament is incompatible with the Human Rights Act, and therefore request that the court issue a declaration of incompatibility (see *A and Others v Home Secretary* (2004)). **[Here the issue is not addressed in the form of a question—though it could have been: 'Can Ral rely on the Human Rights Act 1998 to challenge the restrictions on what he can wear, and so request the court to issue a declaration of incompatibility?']**

[Again, the relevant law is introduced and subsequently applied. Note, however, that in the following paragraph the general position regarding the Human Rights Act is set out. In subsequent paragraphs two specific challenges under the Act are identified: (i) Art 9, ECHR ('freedom of religion'); and (ii) Art 10 ECHR ('freedom of expression').] The Human Rights Act 1998 (HRA) has incorporated the bulk of the European Convention on Human Rights 1950 (ECHR) into British law. The HRA places judges under a duty to ensure that '[s]o far as it is possible to do so' legislation is interpreted in a way that is compatible with the ECHR (s 3, HRA). In performing this duty, British judges can take into account the previous case law of both the European Court and the European Commission of Human Rights (s 2), and should a judge hold that UK law is inconsistent with the ECHR, they have the power to issue a declaration of incompatibility (s 4).

[(i) Art 9(1) ECHR]

In seeking to challenge the Protection of Workers Act 2006 which prohibits him from wearing his kap, Ral could seek to argue that the ban on his religious dress constitutes a violation of Art 9(1) of the ECHR. This provision guarantees the right to manifest one's religion or belief 'in worship, teaching, practice or observance'. However, under Art 9(2) the state is justified in interfering with a citizen's rights in this respect, provided three criteria are satisfied:

- First, it must be shown that the curbs on Ral's actions are 'prescribed by law'—here the restrictions on Ral's kap have been introduced by an Act of Parliament.

- Secondly, any restriction on a manifestation of religion or belief must have a legitimate aim— here the State has a legitimate interest in protecting construction workers from dangers inherent in the construction industry, such as matters relating to health and safety.

- Thirdly, the court will have to consider whether the 2006 Act is 'necessary in a democratic society'. The European Court defined this term to mean that there must a 'pressing social need' for the restriction (*Dudgeon v UK* (1981))—in view of the above concerns about protecting construction workers, the State's curbs on headwear are unlikely to be a disproportionate restriction on individual freedom.

A UK court has the discretion to take into account the fact that in an earlier case in Strasbourg (*X v UK* (1977)), the European Commission of Human Rights rejected an application submitted by a Sikh motor cyclist, who claimed that road traffic legislation compelling him to wear a crash helmet (and not his turban) whilst riding a motorcycle, contravened Art 9(2) of the ECHR. The European Commission held that the compulsory wearing of crash helmets was a necessary safety measure for motor cyclists, and that any interference with the individual's freedom of religion was justified as necessary for the protection of health (Art 9(2), ECHR).

Whilst British judges are not strictly bound by previous decisions of the European Court or the now defunct Commission of Human Rights, such a ruling is certainly likely to influence the UK courts and will militate against Ral's chances of success under Art 9 of the ECHR.

[(ii) Art 10, ECHR]

Equally, it would be difficult for Ral to invoke the principle of freedom of expression (Art 10). Not only is it unclear whether wearing a kap would constitute 'expression' for the purposes of Art 10(1), but even if it did, the same kinds of arguments discussed above could be used to justify limits on freedom of expression (Art 10(2)). Thus, it is unlikely that Ral would be able to rely upon Art 10, ECHR to challenge the ban on the wearing of his kap.

In conclusion, in weighing up Ral's respective arguments, there is little doubt that his case for challenging the Protection of Workers Act 2006 is much stronger under EC law than under the Human Rights Act.

Analysis

(a) This question raises a number of different points that clearly need to be dealt with in some sort of logical order. In so doing, the answer differentiates between whether Ral can rely on the EC Regulation and whether he can successfully rely upon the Human Rights Act 1998. As has been stressed throughout this book, it is imperative that your answer is structured clearly. Failure to do so can lead to major problems especially in a question such as this, where students sometimes mix up EC institutions (e.g. the European Commission and the European Court of Justice) and those organs responsible for the interpretation of the European Convention on Human Rights (e.g. the European Court of Human Rights and the now dissolved European Commission of Human Rights). A clear structure reduces the likelihood of such problems occurring.

(b) The IRAC method, explained earlier, has also been used in this answer. It can be illustrated if we look at whether Ral can rely on the Regulation in order to challenge the Act of Parliament. In the first paragraph, the answer identifies the main issue. The relevant rules of law are then covered in the next two paragraphs, with paragraph 1 focusing on the position in Europe and paragraph 2 concentrating on that in the UK. Having explained the law in detail, paragraph 3 demonstrates its application to the relevant facts, and the answer goes on to analyse Ral's other legal options (e.g. the Human Rights Act 1998), rounding off with the conclusion that Ral will almost certainly be able to rely on the EC Regulation.

(c) As mentioned earlier in this book, resist the temptation to be led by cases (see pp 22–24). An answer where every sentence starts off with the words, 'In the case of . . . ', or in which unnecessary time is devoted to the facts of a case, suggests that you are being controlled by the material rather than vice versa. Note, that while a considerable number of cases are cited, it is only the constitutionally significant *R v Secretary of State for Transport, ex p Factortame Ltd (No 2)* [1991] 1AC 603 which warrants detailed analysis.

(d) Following on from what was said in Chapter 1 about getting down to the job at hand as quickly as possible (see pp 5–6), it is worth pointing out that the answer does not waste time dwelling on irrelevant issues. For example, when students answer questions on EC law, some spend a disproportionate amount of time writing long introductions about the history or institutions of the European Union. In answering the kind of question above, such an introduction is simply unnecessary. Similarly, the answer does not waste words describing the Human Rights Act 1998. Instead, it focuses directly on how R may invoke the 1998 Act to achieve redress.

Note

It is also important to appreciate that also not every problem question in the area of constitutional law will focus on *legal* issues. As we have seen, certain principles which underpin the British constitution—e.g. constitutional conventions, the rule of law—are essentially political rather than legal. Accordingly, political remedies are often as important to individuals with grievances as those formally provided by the courts. This is the case, for example, when facing a problem question on devolution, ministerial responsibility, or a hung Parliament. Without the reassuring safety net of a series of legal rules to rely on, some students feel intimidated. Yet, in such areas, the techniques which have been relied upon throughout the book in relation to strictly legal issues can again be successfully applied to those issues which are essentially political. This is illustrated by the following problem question.

Question

Mandy has been the victim of a serious sexual assault. She was attacked in the street at 2 a.m. after deciding to walk home by herself from a party, following a row with her boyfriend. Mandy was later found dazed and bleeding by a police officer. She was immediately rushed to hospital where she remained for three nights. As a result of the attack she has been receiving specialist counselling for the past six months.

At the High Court trial of her alleged attacker, the judge, Blythe J, sat with his eyes closed for much of the time, and appeared to be paying little interest to the proceedings. In his summing up to the jury, Blythe J addressed the issues and then added: 'Young women should not go out alone late at night. In so doing the victim (who appears not to have suffered any lasting ill effects) was asking for trouble. In this case there has been a great deal of contributory negligence.'

The defendant was later found guilty of the offences with which he had originally been charged, but Mandy is still incensed by the judge's behaviour and comments. She wishes to complain about the judge's actions and comes to you for advice.

Suggested answer

This question concerns judicial accountability. In particular, it raises the issue of whether a High Court judge may be disciplined, or forced to resign or to apologize for comments made during the course of a trial. [**As you can see, the answer starts off by identifying the main issue. The fact that you are to advise Mandy—who wishes to complain about the judge's conduct at the trial—tells us that the question is about the accountability of judges, as opposed, say, to crimes against women.**] High Court judges are appointed by the Crown on the advice of the Lord Chancellor (Supreme Court Act 1981, s 10). They hold office during good behaviour and can only be removed by the Queen after a Resolution is passed by both Houses of Parliament (Supreme Court Act 1981, s 11(3)). Under common law, a judge is immune from liability for anything said in his or her judicial capacity in a court of law (*Scott v Stansfield* (1868)). And, similarly, the Crown is immune from liability for the actions of a judge participating in the judicial process (Crown Proceedings Act 1947, s 2(5)). **[The relevant constitutional rules have been identified and outlined. Note how the answer refers only to High Court judges—this is all that is required. There is no need to discuss how 'inferior judges', such as circuit judges, may be removed from office.]**

Mandy (M) appears to have two separate complaints: that the judge failed to pay proper attention to the case; and that he made inappropriate comments about female victims of crime. In the past judges have been criticized for falling asleep and paying inadequate attention to proceedings in court (*R v Edworthy* (1961)). Similarly the judge's comments about women 'asking for trouble' are inappropriate and arguably incompatible with his holding office 'during good behaviour'.

In seeking redress, M may wish to draw public attention to the judge's comments about women, while at the same time preserving her anonymity. Thus she might wish to enlist the support of a pressure group (e.g. a women's group). **[This suggestion reveals a degree of practical insight which, if combined with academic ability, will be noted by the examiner and duly rewarded.]** M and her supporters appear to have at least two political options open to them.

The first option is to petition the Lord Chancellor who could, with the agreement of the Lord Chief Justice, suspend the judge (Constitutional Reforms Act 2005, s 108(5)). A much more likely remedy however would be for the Lord Chief Justice and the Lord Chancellor to quietly censure the judge. Private pressure of this type might lead Blythe J to apologize or agree that he will no longer hear any more cases involving sex crimes (e.g. in 1993 Prosser J agreed not to try any more rape cases after his remark that the teenage victim of a rape should be given £500 by her attacker for a holiday, caused a public furore). However, if the Lord Chancellor and Lord Chief Justice consider that the judicial misconduct is particularly serious, they could issue a formal public rebuke. The Lord Chancellor issued such a statement in 1982 after a trial judge's comment that a female hitch hiker (who had been raped) was contributorily negligent. Admittedly, it is rare for a Lord Chancellor or Lord Chief Justice to censure a judge publicly, yet such a course of action could lead to Blythe J's resignation, or might facilitate his removal from office by Parliament.

The second option is to seek to have the judge dismissed by Parliament for misconduct. M should therefore seek to contact sympathetic MPs (though not Ministers, who by convention are expected to refrain from criticizing judges or their decisions). It is a Parliamentary rule that individual backbench MPs may criticize judges only when debating a substantive critical motion. Thus a successful campaign by M's supporters might lead to the introduction of a motion calling for the dismissal of Blythe J.

The chances of this option succeeding are, however, slim. The last judge to have been removed from office by means of a resolution from both Houses was Jonah Barrington in 1830. In that case Barrington had misappropriated money and at the time of the resolution had effectively retired as a judge. Moreover, even if a resolution were to be proposed in Parliament, precise charges would need to be formulated; and in the absence of any clear precedents these charges could prove difficult to draft. In addition, since the issue here is Blythe J's removal from office, the judge would need to be afforded the opportunity to have a fair hearing in accordance with the rules of natural justice (*Ridge v Baldwin* (1964, HL)). The whole process would, therefore, be both time-consuming and expensive. [**In this part of the answer, the relevant rules have been applied to the facts of the case. It is suggested that M may obtain redress from two possible sources: the Lord Chancellor/Lord Chief Justice and Parliament. Although there is very little statutory authority or case law in this area, there are still plenty of authorities to support the answer.**]

In conclusion, despite the obvious difficulties in proceeding, M and her supporters (including presumably the media) might succeed in exerting sufficient pressure on Blythe J to force him to apologize or resign (and certainly to discourage him from making similar remarks in future). [**This is a simple conclusion: it ties together some of the points which were made earlier. It is also practical in that it notes that M's chances of success ultimately depend on her availing herself of political remedies.**]

As noted earlier, whether you will need to tackle a problem question dealing with the principles of the British constitution will very much depend on the emphasis of your public law course. Your course co-ordinator will be able to tell you about the sorts of questions you can legitimately expect to encounter in your exam.

2   Civil liberties

A typical civil liberties question to be found on public law exam papers will involve the topic of police powers. When considering such questions, it would be advisable to keep the following questions at the forefront of your mind:

- Has the police officer a legal power to act in this situation? If so, what does the power consist of (i.e. is it statute-based, e.g. Police and Criminal Evidence Act (PACE) 1984, or is it a common law power, e.g. breach of the peace)?
- If the police officer has a power to act, are they lawfully exercising that power? (Note how often in PACE 1984, a police officer's power is limited by the proviso that it must be exercised reasonably.)
- What safeguards does the individual have? For example, outside the police station, when a stop and search is made, the police officer is under an obligation to convey certain information to the suspect (s 2(2), (3), PACE 1984). Similarly, inside the police station the individual has the right to consult privately with a lawyer (s 58, PACE 1984).
- Has the suspect any remedies (e.g. a subsequent civil action, for assault, false imprisonment, etc.)?

These questions can also be used as a 'micro structure' around which the IRAC method can be woven.

Question

PC Dibble and PC Duff are on a foot patrol at 3 a.m., in a residential area of Grampton. They receive a call to attend a dispute at a nearby house. As they approach the house, they hear a lot of shouting and screaming, and the sound of breaking glass. The front door is open, and as they walk up to it they are confronted by Rocky, who is six foot tall and of a muscular build. He is very angry, smells strongly of alcohol, and screams at them that they are not entering his house. Cowering behind him is Walter, who has two black eyes, ripped clothing, a bleeding nose, and is in a state of distress. Walter invites the officers into the house, saying that he would like to talk to them. The officers try to push past Rocky. He objects, picks up PC Dibble and throws him into the garden, as a result of which Dibble receives severe bruising. PC Duff summons assistance, and within seconds a van load of officers arrive and drag Rocky into the van, injuring his face in the process. PC Duff tells him that he is taking him to the police station 'to help with enquiries', and he is driven away in the police van.

Suddenly Angie, Rocky's girlfriend, appears from the house. She stands in the road in front of the police van, preventing it from moving and screaming and shouting obscenities at the top of her voice. PC Duff warns her to desist or else she will be arrested. Angie continues to scream. Soon a number of lights come on in nearby houses and it is obvious that she has woken some of her neighbours. Angie is arrested and placed in the police van.

Meanwhile PC Duff returns to the house and searches every room in case 'there is anything that could be evidence'. As a result of the search, he finds a minute quantity of cannabis in Rocky's bedroom.
Discuss.

Suggested answer

The entry of the police officers and Rocky's response

[Using the IRAC method, the first issue is addressed:] The first issue is whether the police may lawfully enter the house. A critical factor in this respect is whether Walter has the authority to invite the officers inside. **[Next, the relevant rules of law relating to common law powers of entry are explained:]** At common law a police officer may enter premises with the express or implied permission of the owner (*Davis v Lisle* (1936)). If Walter is the owner/occupier, the entry is lawful. Similarly, entry is permissible if Walter and Rocky are joint owners/occupiers (*R v Thornley* (1981)). And, <u>equally</u>, if Walter is a co-occupier, he is able to grant entry to the police (*R v Lamb* (1990)).

Irrespective of the above, the police have a common law power to enter public or private premises to prevent or deal with a breach of the peace: the rule in *Thomas v Sawkins* (1935), retained in s 17(6) Police and Criminal Evidence Act (PACE) 1984. Mere rowdiness of itself will not constitute a breach of the peace—instead breach of the peace is limited to situations where violence has occurred or the likelihood of it occurring is imminent (*R v Howell* (1981)).

[Application of the law to the facts, and conclusion:] Walter's black eyes, torn clothes and bleeding nose demonstrate that violence (a prerequisite of the offence of breach of the peace) has occurred. The fact that this violence took place in a private home is no defence, since a breach of the peace can take place on private premises for the purpose of entitling a constable on reasonable grounds to make an arrest (*McConnell v CC Greater Manchester* (1990)). And a police officer has an independent right under common law to remain on premises if they reasonably anticipate a breach of the peace on those premises (*Lamb v DPP* (1989)). Walter's condition, plus the sounds of shouting, screaming, and breaking glass, appear to provide the police officers with reasonable grounds to act in these circumstances.

[A new 'issue' is then introduced:] In addition to their common law powers, the police officers may seek to rely on s 17, PACE 1984. **[The issue here is, of course, whether the police officers may in fact do so. The relevant rules relating to this point are then outlined:]** They seem to have a number of options. First, as mentioned earlier, the police retain their power of entry to prevent a breach of the peace (s 17(6)). Secondly, relying on s 17(1)(e), the police officers might argue that they wish to enter the premises to save life or limb (e.g. Walter's), or to prevent serious damage to property due to Rocky's enraged state (e.g. breaking glass). Thirdly, it is possible that the police have a power of entry under s 17(1)(b) to arrest for an indictable offence, as defined in s 24, PACE 1984. This would be exercisable (s 17(2)(a)) only if the police had reasonable grounds for believing that the person they were seeking (here Rocky) was on the premises. (On the facts he was). **[Having set out the relevant law, it is now applied to the facts of the problem question:]** In view of Walter's black eyes, bleeding nose, ripped clothing, and distressed state, it appears that there may have been an assault, occasioning actual bodily harm (s 47, Offences Against the Persons Act (OAPA) 1861) or grievous bodily harm (s 20, OAPA 1861). The police might also seek to invoke the powers of arrest under s 24(2), PACE 1984 which states that where a constable has 'reasonable grounds for suspecting that an offence has been committed', s/he may arrest anyone who s/he has reasonable grounds to suspect of being guilty of it. Blood on Rocky's hands would appear to suggest guilt, and the test for reasonable grounds is objective (*Castorina v CC of Surrey* (1988).

[The following section hints at a conclusion, but introduces new material regarding the nature of the arrest:] These powers, read with the facts, tend to suggest that the entry of the police officers is lawful. Thus, assuming that the officers are acting lawfully, Rocky's actions may mean that he has assaulted a constable in the execution of his duty, contrary to s 89(1), Police Act 1996. However, on being arrested Rocky must be informed of the fact and the grounds for the arrest, either at the time, or as soon as possible thereafter (s 28, PACE 1984). It should have been made clear to Rocky that he was being arrested (*R v Brosch* (1988)), so that merely being told that he is 'helping with enquiries' is too vague.

[Finally, a conclusion is offered:] Since he has been unlawfully detained, Rocky may be entitled to use reasonable force to escape (*Kenlin v Gardiner* (1967)). Picking up PC Dibble and throwing him into the garden certainly does not seem to be reasonable. What is less clear is whether the officers used reasonable force in restraining Rocky, who is tall and well built. The 'dragging' of Rocky and the injury to his face suggests that unreasonable force was used and certainly indicates that his attendance at the police station was not voluntary: s 29, PACE 1984.

The arrest of Angie

[Another new issue is introduced. Note, how in this section of the answer, that a much more direct approach is taken regarding the setting out of the law and its application to the facts:] The next issue to be discussed concerns whether Angie can be lawfully arrested. Angie has been arrested for shouting in a residential area in the middle of the night. The grounds for arrest could be behaviour 'within the hearing or sight' of people 'likely to be caused harassment, alarm or distress' (Public Order Act (POA) 1986, s 5(1)). The fact that lights come on in nearby houses might indicate that this is established. And even if only the police officers witnessed Angie screaming then, according to *DPP v Orum* (1988), they too are capable of being caused harassment, alarm, or distress for the purposes of s 5. Thus, Angie may be arrested under POA 1986, s 5(4). She is unlikely to be able to rely on the two available defences to this offence: (i) that she lacks *mens rea* (s 6(4)) (there is no indication that she does); and (ii) that her behaviour is reasonable (s 5(3)(c)) (screaming obscenities at 3 a.m. in a residential district seems unreasonable). By standing in front of the police van in the road, Angie may also be wilfully obstructing the highway (Highways Act 1980, s 137). However, it is more likely that Angie is committing the offence of willfully obstructing a police officer in the execution of his/her duty (Police Act 1996, s 89(2), for which the officers have the power to arrest for obstruction (*Wershof v MPC* (1978)).

The search of the house

Another issue to be discussed is whether by returning to the house and searching it, PC Duff is acting illegally. A police officer may enter a house by warrant, statute, or consent. There is no evidence that it has been authorized by a warrant (s 8, PACE 1984), or by Walter. And even presupposing that Walter has sufficient authority, his consent must be given in writing before the search takes place, with the police officer satisfied that Walter is in a position to give consent (Code B, 5.1). Since this has not happened, the entry would appear to be prima facie unlawful. In addition, the breach of the Code may affect the admissibility of the cannabis seized in later court proceedings (s 67(10), PACE 1984) and the court may choose to exclude it (s 78, PACE 1984).

Neither can PC Duff's entry be justified under s 18, PACE 1984. This section provides that an officer can enter premises only if there are reasonable grounds for suspecting that there is evidence present in relation to an offence they are investigating. It is difficult to see how this might be the case in the problem; and even if such a search were permitted, it has not been authorized in writing by an officer of at least the rank of inspector (s 18(4), PACE 1984).

Presumably PC Duff seizes the cannabis under s 19(3), PACE 1984 to prevent it from being concealed or destroyed. However, he must have been lawfully in the house to seize any items (s 19(1), PACE 1984). Since this is in doubt, Rocky will hope that the court will exercise its discretion under s 78, PACE 1984, to exclude the evidence of the minute quantity of cannabis, on the ground that it was unfairly obtained (*R v Khan* (1997) AC 558).

Irrespective of the success of this argument, Rocky may consider bringing a number of civil actions against the police. The failure lawfully to arrest Rocky could lead to a civil action for false imprisonment. Moreover the fact that unreasonable force was used in his detention could also provide the basis for a civil action for assault. Finally, an action may lie for trespass to property (in relation to the later, unlawful search). In relation to these civil actions Rocky would sue the Chief Constable of the force, but any damages would be paid by his Police Authority (s 88(3), Police Act 1996).

Lastly, even if these actions are not successful, Rocky and Angie could complain to the Independent Police Complaints Commission about the actions of the officers in this scenario (Police Reform Act 2002). This could lead to disciplinary charges being brought against those officers who flouted the rules in PACE 1984 and the Code of Practice.

Analysis

(a) In order to answer this question, a student must first decide whether the police officers have the power to enter the house. The answer highlights three possibilities:

- the right of a co-occupier or joint owner to grant permission;
- common law police powers to enter to deal with a breach of the peace;
- PACE 1984, s 17.

The first possibility is the most obvious. The fact that Walter is in the house at 3 a.m. would imply that he resides there (it may also be significant that the door is open and were this not his house Walter might have 'escaped'). On the other hand, Rocky refers to it as 'his house' and the drugs are found in 'Rocky's bedroom'. Further speculation is unnecessary. Instead, cite the relevant case law, drawing out any noteworthy facts. The details in the question are left deliberately vague. It is, therefore, entirely legitimate to discuss the other options available to the police in deciding whether they can lawfully enter the house.

The second possibility, is the power of the police to prevent or to deal with a breach of the peace. The fact that most public law textbooks deal with the breach of the peace in their chapters on public order (and not in the police powers sections) occasionally deceives a few students into thinking that breach of the peace could not possibly be relevant in a question which is ostensibly on police powers. Such an idea is fallacious and shows the danger of ignoring 'the big picture'. As you will have observed, significant public order issues arise later in the question. This should serve as a warning to 'question spotters'. If you gamble on leaving out an area of your course—always a dangerous option—try to ensure that it is unrelated to those areas on which you are hoping to rely.

The third possibility, is that the police officers may rely upon other subsections in s 17, PACE 1984 to enter the house. The sheer length of s 17 can intimidate some students and it is not unknown for the weaker ones (who, while in the exam hall, have the benefit of a statute book containing PACE 1984) to copy out large parts of s 17 without detailed explanation. Not surprisingly, such a course of action is unproductive. As noted earlier, where a statute book is provided, you will not receive credit for repeating the relevant statutory section—in fact all that you are doing is drawing your lack of knowledge to the examiner's attention. Instead, relate the appropriate statutory provisions to the facts of the question.

(b) The main advantage of 'cracking open' the question by way of the four question 'micro structure' outlined above is that it ensures that your material is presented in a logical fashion. Students are often tempted to abandon any form of structure in the rush to put pen to paper. Of course, on occasion, flexibility is required. From the above answer, you will have noticed that the first two questions of the suggested micro structure—the existence of a power and the use of that power—overlap. In the same way, the last two questions (i.e. the individual's safeguards and remedies) tend to cross over. For example, in this scenario, s 28, PACE 1984 (information to be conveyed on arrest) appears not to have been complied with. Because Rocky has not been given the grounds and reason for his arrest, the police officers lose the shield of the law. Thus Rocky can bring a civil action for false imprisonment, seeking damages from the period when first detained to the time he was notified of his arrest. Similarly, the fact that the police officers 'drag Rocky into the van, injuring his face in the process', suggests the use of unreasonable force and an action for assault. The principle of vicarious liability means that the Chief Constable of the relevant force will be the defendant. These are rather obvious points, but it is surprising how many students fail to raise them. One possible explanation is that many examinees assume that since such civil actions come within the framework of the law of tort, they could not possibly be relevant in a public law exam. Of course, a detailed analysis of the possible tortious issues is not necessary, yet civil actions are often seen as providing effective remedies to which individuals aggrieved by police misconduct may resort. Your inclusion of this issue will suggest that you have a good overall understanding of public law.

(c) The introduction of Angie into the problem question raises issues of public order law. Note how the answer did not limit itself solely to the Public Order Act 1986. Instead it draws upon the two other sources of law relevant to this area: common law powers (e.g. breach of the peace), and other statutory powers (e.g. Highways Act 1980). Nevertheless, the Public Order Act 1986 is an important piece of legislation and if you answer a question on this area you must have a good working knowledge of it (as well as statutes such as the Criminal Justice and Public Order Act 1994, which were not relevant for the purposes of the present question). Here a competent student will identify the power of arrest—it is significant that Angie was arrested only after the police officer told her to stop screaming and swearing, and warned her that she could be arrested. This satisfies s 5(4), Public Order Act 1986, which provides that where a police officer warns a person to cease engaging in 'offensive conduct' and that person fails to stop, the police officer then has the power to make an arrest.

(d) Lastly, since some of the facts in this question are unclear, the suggested answer raises a number of different possibilities. It can reasonably be assumed that the examiner deliberately left parts of the question vague, so that the student is free to explore a range of different options. The fact that the question asks you to 'discuss', rather than a more specific instruction, (e.g. advise Rocky), would tend to confirm this.

3 Judicial review

One possible strategy, or micro structure, in approaching judicial review problem questions is to start thinking about the question by asking yourself five questions:

- Is this the decision of a body which is, in principle, subject to judicial review (i.e., is it a public law matter)?
- If so, has the applicant complied with the procedural requirements for judicial review (e.g. locus standi, time limits, etc.)?
- What basis (if any) is there for seeking judicial review on the grounds of illegality, irrationality and procedural impropriety?
- Are there any grounds for judicial review under the Human Rights Act 1998?
- What legal remedies may the applicant invoke?

As discussed later, you do not necessarily need to address these questions in the exact order suggested above. However, they would need to be addressed somewhere in your answer, albeit that some would be given greater emphasis than others (much will depend on the nature of the public law course you are studying). The following question employs the above micro structure to good effect:

Question

An Act of Parliament has granted local authorities the power to acquire land compulsorily to build sports facilities in areas where there is a 'definite need' for these facilities. Any such action can only be taken under this Act after a period of public consultation following a majority vote of councillors in a full council meeting. It must also be subject to the approval of the Minister for Sport.

In February 2006, Frank received notice that Greytown District Council Planning Committee had decided that his house was to be compulsorily purchased and demolished to facilitate the building of a large leisure complex, which was to include an Olympic-size swimming pool. The Minister for Sport approved the proposed development.

Frank complains that there is already an indoor swimming pool three miles from his house. While this pool is not of Olympic size, it is busy only at weekends. Frank also wonders if it is relevant that the son of the Chairman of the Council, who is a well-known swimmer, published a letter in a local paper a year earlier, in which he complained that he had difficulty training as there were no Olympic-size swimming pools in that area.
Advise Frank.

Suggested answer

Judicial review is available only where public law issues are concerned. Frank (F) is fortunate that in this scenario the administrative authorities (the council and the Minister) are clearly public law bodies. Accordingly, there is a prima facie case for judicial review. To seek judicial review, the applicant must comply with certain procedural requirements. For example F's application must be brought within three months from the date on which the decision he is seeking to challenge was taken (CPR, Part 54.5(1)). In addition, the applicant must have a 'sufficient interest' in the matter to which the application relates (CPR, 54.2)). Because it is F's house that is to be purchased, prima facie F would appear to have standing. Assuming F has satisfied the requisite procedural requirements, the court will then turn to examine the basis for F's claim for judicial review. **[The above material deals with the first two questions set out in the above microstructure and provides a signpost indicating that the answer will move on to the third and fourth questions—the grounds for review.]**

In *CCSU v Minister for Civil Service* (1985) (hereinafter the *GCHQ* case), Lord Diplock defined the grounds for judicial review using a threefold classification of illegality, procedural impropriety, and irrationality.

Illegality

Illegality covers situations where administrative authorities have made jurisdictional errors or have acted *ultra vires*. Here F could claim that the local authority (LA) has exceeded its powers and has acted *ultra vires* (illegally) in two respects. F could ground his claim in substantive *ultra vires*. The Act enables the LA compulsorily to acquire land to build sports facilities only. However, the LA proposes to construct a leisure complex. F could, therefore, argue that this is a different enterprise from that provided for in the Act. Since 'leisure' could be construed to imply the construction of shops, cinemas, and restaurants, this may mean that the LA is exceeding the power delegated to it by the statute (*A-G v Fulham Corp* (1921)). The LA, on the other hand, could contend that a leisure complex is reasonably incidental to the legislation (*A-G v Great Eastern Railway* (1880)). However, F could respond that the 'reasonably incidental' principle tends to be narrowly construed (*McCarthy and Stone v Richmond* (1991, HL)).

Secondly, F may claim that there has been an unauthorized delegation of power. This is the principle that where a statute grants a power to a particular administrative body, that authority may not be delegated to another, unless provided for or authorized by the Act of Parliament (*Barnard v National Dock Labour Board* (1953, CA)). Therefore F could argue that the LA has improperly delegated its power to its planning committee. The LA may, however, respond by pointing out that local government councils have long had wide powers to delegate their functions to committees and sub-committees. The legitimacy of this delegation will ultimately turn on the actual wording of the Act.

Procedural impropriety

In determining whether to review a decision on the ground of procedural impropriety (e.g. a public body's non-compliance with a specific procedural requirement) the courts will typically take into account all of the circumstances of the case (*R v Secretary of State for Social Services, ex p AMA* (1986)). F should therefore argue that since there is no indication that the LA has either complied with the specific procedure in the act of ensuring public consultation, or ensured that the compulsory purchase has been authorized by a majority vote of councillors in a full council meeting, the relevant decisions can be challenged on the basis of procedural impropriety. Given that F risks being deprived of a fundamental right (e.g. losing his home), the failure to consult and comply with the statutory procedure means that the LA's decision should be set aside (*Lee v Des* (1967)). This is a strong argument, and it is difficult to see how the LA could convincingly raise a defence that F is not prejudiced by the LA's non-compliance with the procedural requirements.

Procedural impropriety also includes judge-made rules of procedural fairness and natural justice. Thus, even if F is unsuccessful in making the above submission, he could seek to base his claim on his right to 'natural justice'. Traditionally the courts divided the rules of natural justice into two categories: (i) the rule against bias; and (ii) the right to a fair hearing. Notwithstanding the fact that the courts tend now to emphasize a duty to act fairly (*Ridge v Baldwin* (1964, HL)), F may seek to rely on the traditional two principles of natural justice.

The fact that the son of the council Chairman is a keen swimmer who has publicly called for the construction of an Olympic-size swimming pool, obviously creates the impression of bias. F should therefore seek to rely on the principle that 'justice may not only be done but should . . . be seen to be done' (Lord Hewart in *R v Sussex Justices, ex p McCarthy* (1924)). As a man of rank, the council Chairman could unfairly influence council policy (*Metropolitan Properties Ltd v Lannon* (1969)), even if he took no part in the council's decision (*R v Hendon RDC, ex p Chorley* (1933)). Therefore, there is a 'real possibility' that a 'fair-minded and informed observer' would conclude that the decision-maker had been biased (*Porter v Magill* (2002)). Unless the council can show—e.g. that it was council policy to build the complex long before the Chairman took his position and his son wrote the letter, or it can be demonstrated that the Chairman had no actual influence over council policy—there would appear to be bias.

Since F's house is to be demolished for the construction of the new complex, he can also argue that he should be accorded a fair hearing (*Cooper v Wandsworth Board of Works* (1863)). On the facts, there is no indication that F has been given this opportunity. The right to a fair hearing should depend on the consequences of the decision to the individual (*Ridge v Baldwin*). Normally neither an oral hearing nor legal representation are automatic ingredients of a fair hearing (*R v Board of Visitors, Maze Prison, ex p Hone* (1988)). However, F could argue that since he has a lot to lose, he should be accorded additional rights, because the test for fairness depends on the circumstances of every case (*Lloyd v McMahon* (1987)).

Irrationality

As well as illegality and procedural impropriety, F can challenge the decision to demolish his house on the ground of irrationality. F can argue that: (i) there is no 'definite need' for either an Olympic pool or such a complex; (ii) no reasonable council would embark on such an enterprise when there is already a pool in the locality (*Wednesbury* (1948)); and (iii) such a decision is perverse and lacks logic (*GCHQ* case (1984)).

The council might try to justify its decision on the ground that the existing pool is unsafe or too small to cater for local needs, while Frank could respond that this course of action was irrational, given that they could have refurbished and expanded the existing pool. Ultimately the legitimacy of this decision will turn on the facts. Thus, if the LA can show that its new complex is being designed to respond to a population increase (e.g. new housing estates are being built or new businesses are coming to the area) then that may well be enough to rebut the presumption that the decision is unreasonable. Whilst the courts are usually slow to strike down administrative decisions as irrational (Lord Diplock in *GCHQ*), F can also be reassured that the more substantial the interference with one's human rights, the greater the level of scrutiny that is required by the courts (Lord Bingham in *R v Ministry of Defence, ex p Smith* (1996)).

The Human Rights Act 1998 (HRA)

Public authorities are under a legal obligation to take decisions or pursue policies that are not incompatible with the ECHR (s 6, HRA). The council is clearly a public authority for these purposes. F could argue that, as a result of the compulsorily purchase and the demolition of his house, he is being deprived of his right to property (Art 1, Protocol 1 of the ECHR). As a result of the fact this right is not absolute, the central issue is likely to be whether the interference with F's property rights is proportionate (*R v Home Secretary, ex p Daly* (2001)). Given that the loss of his home is a substantial interference with his human rights, F can therefore make a strong case for the review of this decision (*R v Ministry of Defence, ex p Smith* (1996)).

Remedies

Having invoked these grounds for review, it seems very likely that F's legal challenge will be successful. While remembering that public law remedies are discretionary, F would be well advised to seek a prohibiting order (preventing the LA from compulsorily purchasing his house). This would ensure that in the meantime his house is not demolished (*AG v Fulham Corp* (1921)). Since the Planning Committee has already taken the decision to purchase and demolish his house, F should also seek a quashing order to quash the decision (as opposed to a prohibiting order which is sought to prevent such actions). F may also seek a declaration that the Committee's decision to make the order is null and void. While not legally enforceable, such declarations are usually obeyed and have been issued in response to unreasonable planning conditions (*Hall v Shoreham UDC* (1964)).

Lastly it should be observed that if F was unsuccessful in seeking leave to apply for judicial review, he has two further remedies: he could contact the Parliamentary Commissioner for

Administration concerning the Minister's approval of the proposed development (Parliamentary Commissioner for Administration Act 1967, s 5), or the Commissioners for Local Administration (Local Government Act 1974, s 26) who investigate complaints of local authority maladministration.

Analysis

You should consider the following points in planning how to answer a judicial review problem question:

(a) The suggested five-part micro structure to be applied in questions of this type, will provide a useful model for marshalling your arguments. The ordering is not accidental, since *in practice* it is critical that certain issues are dealt with at the preliminary stage—e.g. whether the applicant has standing to submit a claim for judicial review. In other words, even if an applicant has been adversely affected by a decision which is obviously illegal or irrational, the applicant will fail to obtain redress if they are unable to satisfy the standing, or indeed any other procedural, requirements. Broadly speaking, this approach has been adopted in the answer above. Of course, problem questions are not primarily about practice. They are *academic exercises* and it would be entirely legitimate to leave procedural matters such as standing until the end of your answer. This is especially so if, had they been considered earlier in your answer, the only feasible conclusion you could have come to would have been that F did not have standing. Such an approach would have resulted in a premature exit from the question and a corresponding loss of marks.

(b) So what overall proportion of your answer should be devoted to each part of the five-question model? Ultimately the weight which you attach to these areas will depend on both the wording of the problem question you are answering and its instructions. Here guidance is provided by the facts of the question, because the decision has been taken by a Minister and a local authority. Since there is no uncertainty about whether the relevant administrative authority is a public law body or whether it is exercising a public function (see *R v Panel on Take-Overs and Mergers, ex p Datafin plc* [1987] 1 All ER 564), you should avoid a detailed analysis of what exactly amounts to a public law issue. It is simply not necessary on the facts. Similarly, the close connection between Frank and the compulsory purchase and demolition of his house, suggests that satisfying the *locus standi* requirement is not a problem. Again, anything other than a brief reference to this would be unnecessary. Lastly, since the question does not ask for a description or an analysis of the procedure to be employed when applying for judicial review, its inclusion is superfluous. Avoid unnecessary background information. Students who start their answers with a disproportionately long introduction, charting, for example, the history of the Supreme Court Act 1981, or merely describing the new Civil Procedure Rules (CPR 54), can expect little credit. These answers are more likely to irritate than impress the examiner.

(c) In answering this question, we have employed Lord Diplock's three 'i's test in the *GCHQ* case. It is a useful tool—a sort of 'legal umbrella'—which prior to the Human Rights Act 1998 categorized the different grounds for review. As you may have observed when studying judicial review, the classification may be tidy, but it is not perfect. Cases frequently arise which fall into more than one of Lord Diplock's categories and some academics dislike the test as it may erroneously imply (especially in the wake of the Human Rights Act 1998) that there are only three ways of challenging administrative action. Common sense dictates that if the lecturer on your course has an aversion to Lord Diplock's classification you may be advised to adopt their approach. However, whatever approach you adopt (and the suggested answer adopts the first one), make sure that you identify and analyse the different grounds for review. Certainly, the alliteration of Lord Diplock's test (the three 'i's), makes it easy to remember; and the fact that the House of Lords subsequently endorsed it (*R v Secretary of State for the Environment, ex p Hammersmith and Fulham LBC* [1991] 1 AC 521), makes it not merely a useful, but also an authoritative method for handling the grounds of judicial review.

Having identified the grounds for review, you should identify Frank's remedies. It is important to match your remedies to the facts and the legal issues generated in the question. Sometimes weak students will just list the remedies (e.g. mandatory, prohibiting, quashing orders . . .) in note form, without any detailed explanation of which are relevant and why. This 'hit and hope' approach is not likely to fool the examiner. Having identified the appropriate remedies, you should point out that all public law remedies (with the exception of damages) are discretionary—for example, the motives of the applicant may be relevant (*R v Commissioners of Customs and Excise, ex p Cook* [1970] 1 WLR 450)—so that there is no right to a remedy, irrespective of the strength of the merits of his or her case.

(d) In answering these questions, always bear in mind the nature of judicial review. Judicial review is the power of the High Court to supervise the actions of government bodies by applying public law principles. Thus it is important not to confuse or misuse the terms 'appeal' and 'review'. There are significant differences. Appeal proceedings enable the court to change the decision of the body appealed from in a particular case (e.g. in tort, an appeal court can increase the sum of damages to be awarded to the victim of an accident caused by the defendant's negligence). However, review means that the court has only a supervisory jurisdiction (e.g. the supervising court cannot take decisions, it can only quash illegal decisions). Unlike an appeal, which gives the court the power to decide whether a decision is 'right or wrong', judicial review empowers a court only to review whether the relevant legal rules for arriving at a decision were correctly applied in the circumstances of the case. Therefore the student who writes 'Frank should appeal for judicial review', is revealing his or her lack of knowledge and understanding of this area.

(e) Remember that there are some factors, not so far covered, which may restrict the court's powers of review. Obvious examples of things to look out for are public interest immunity certificates and ouster clauses. Similarly, the reports of the Parliamentary Commissioner for Administration have been held by judges to be immune from review (*R v PCA, ex p Dyer* [1994] 1 All ER 375). The fact that none of these areas is relevant to the problem at hand should not detract from their potential importance to any judicial review question you might later have to answer.

(f) It is axiomatic that a number of judicial review cases are politically controversial. The courts have been asked to answer politically sensitive questions such as: Can the government detain, without trial, non-British nationals suspected of being involved in terrorism (*A and Others v Home Secretary* [2004] UKWL 56)? Can the Spanish owners of fishing vessels force the UK government to allow their ships to fish in British waters pending a ruling from the European Court of Justice (*R v Secretary of State for Transport, ex p Factortame Ltd (No 2)* [1991] 1 AC 603)? Can the Home Secretary lawfully ban the transmission of words spoken by members of Sinn Fein and other proscribed organisations (*R v Secretary of State for the Home Department, ex p Brind* [1991] 1 AC 696)? And, can a woman suffering from motor neurone disease use the Human Rights Act 1998 to argue that the right to life (Art 2, ECHR) also includes the right to assisted suicide (*R (Pretty) v DPP* [2002] 1 All ER 1)? Students invariably have their own political views on such decisions, but even though judges may indirectly evaluate the legitimacy of social and political policies, a judicial review problem question is not the appropriate forum for the expression of political sentiment. Avoid partisan political comment in your answers—it is not that your examiner will necessarily disagree with you, but rather that your comments are unlikely to be relevant. Of course, essay questions on topics such as proportional representation, or the reform of the Monarchy or the House of Lords are essentially political. It is, therefore, inevitable that you will be making explicit political judgements in your answers. However, this is a far cry from being given a licence to engage in soapbox rhetoric or getting side-tracked by party politics. Remember that you are in a law exam, and whatever leeway you have in answering the question, you will be expected to apply the tools of legal reasoning.

4 Summary

- The wide-ranging nature of public law—spanning criminal and civil liability and touching on *political* as well as legal sanctions—suggests that it is very different from the other subjects we have so far considered.

- Be sure to keep clear in your mind the differences between various European institutions.

- Although it is helpful to cite a number of cases in any particular answer, only cases directly on point warrant detailed analysis.

- Problem questions are not primarily about practice. They are *academic exercises*. Accordingly, it is entirely appropriate to give you answer an academic slant. However, this discretion should not be taken as a general licence to ignore *all* practical matters.

- Where there is no, or little, uncertainty about a particular issue, simply outline the relevant law as succinctly as possible and move on to the more 'knotty' points of law. This is where the examiner wants you to focus your efforts and where most of your marks will be earned.

- Avoid partisan political comment in your answers—it is not that your examiner will necessarily disagree with you, but rather that your comments are unlikely to be relevant. You are in a law exam, and whatever leeway you have in answering the question, you will be expected to apply the tools of legal reasoning.

Part B

Essay questions

5 Essay questions

Unlike legal problem solving, all law students will have had the opportunity to practise essay writing at some stage in their academic careers. Yet, despite this, few students seem capable of writing truly engaging essays and even fewer seem prepared to make any changes to the way in which they approach essay writing in order to score first-class marks. Consequently, as with problem solving, a large number of students fail to do justice to their many hours of hard work simply because of their poor, or mediocre, essay technique. Without denying that writing an engaging essay is a difficult skill to master, it is nevertheless our view that the necessary techniques can be learned and that, with practice, they can be put to good effect in exams or in coursework assignments. It is the aim of this chapter to demonstrate the hallmarks of good essay writing and to provide worked examples mainly, though not solely, from criminal law and contract law in order to illustrate these techniques.

The material is presented according to the following structure: (1) interpreting the question posed; (2) devising your argument and structuring your answer; and (3) practising your essay writing skills. A summary of the points covered is listed at the end of the chapter.

1 Interpreting the question posed

Undoubtedly the most common complaint amongst examiners is that students routinely fail to answer the *specific* question set (especially in the context of the traditional three-hour exam where typically four questions must be answered). The fact is that many students—even good ones—have a tendency, no matter how clearly the question is framed, to write a *general* answer on the topic to which the question relates rather than one which is *specifically* directed at the precise wording of the question. It is not uncommon, for example, to find that, where the question requires a discussion of the law on 'common mistake', the student has also included material on 'unilateral mistake'; or for an essay question on murder to contain material on the crime of manslaughter. Such a comprehensive approach is, however, wholly unjustified—unless, that is, some direct comparison of the two categories is specifically invited; or such a comparison is implicit in the actual wording of the question. Most questions have identifiable parameters. If the examiner asks for a discussion of issue X, then confine your remarks to issue X. To do otherwise is to demonstrate that you cannot follow simple instructions.

By the same token, avoid long worthy but waffley introductions, which are again aimed at being comprehensive (or as most students prefer to characterize it—'putting the question in context' or 'setting the scene'). These will rarely help you to answer the question, and are unlikely to impress the examiner.

Despite the fact that the material below has nothing to do with law, the answers that are outlined are designed to illustrate two contrasting *styles* of essay writing:

Question

Why did England win the World Cup in 1966?

Answer A[1]

Football was first played in England as a competitive sport in 1876. Thereafter the popularity of the game developed rapidly, and by 1903 there were 43 clubs in the English football league. Abroad, football was also gaining in popularity and it was not long before an international competition was established in which . . .

Answer B

There are probably four main reasons why England won the World Cup in 1966. First, England had home advantage **[you could usefully cite some statistics supporting this claim, since there is evidence indicating that home advantage gives teams a distinct 'edge' or opponents]**. Secondly, the England manager, Alf Ramsay, was widely regarded as being one of the most tactically astute managers of his day **[secondary sources could prove useful here]**. Thirdly, the England squad contained a formidable blend of skill and aggression **[specific players could be named as examples]**. And finally, England had the lion's share of any luck that was going on the day **[e.g. Assistant Referee adjudging ball to be over the line]**.

Whereas most student answers resemble the style in which Answer A is written, most examiners are looking for an answer written more in the style of Answer B. When writing an exam answer—or indeed any answer—you must learn to 'cut to the chase', and your introduction should be written in such a way as to enable you to do so.

Sometimes students fail to answer the question because they take *an overly literal approach* to the question set. Such difficulties typically surface when the question is in the form of a long and/or difficult quotation, with a 'Discuss', or a 'Do you agree?', tagged on for good measure. In seeking to identify the parameters of such a question, it would, of course, not be wrong (and perhaps even sensible) to underline the key words or phrases in the quotation. However, you need to be careful with such an approach. Analysing the quotation line by line can mean that you fail to give sufficient weight to the overall *gist* of the quotation. This can result in an essay with an odd or jarring tone, which glosses over the main issue or those issues which the examiner really wants you to address. In this, respect, getting the emphasis right is crucial to good essay writing. For example:

Until problems in the relationship between the increasingly politicized civil service and Parliament are resolved, Select Committees will be in a weak position to investigate the activities of central government departments.
Discuss.

Somewhere in your answer, the following issues should be addressed:

- What is the relationship between the civil service and Parliament supposed to be?

---

1. The facts and figures in the above answer are fabricated. Harry McVea would like to thank his colleague, Phil Syrpis, for this example.

- Why might it be said to be increasingly politicized (and what relevance does this have)?
- What powers do Select Committees have to investigate the affairs of central government departments?
- Insofar as they are in a weak position, is that weakness attributable to the problems in the relationship between the civil service and Parliament?
- How might these weaknesses be resolved?

Although points (i)–(v) represent the central issues raised by the question, they should be covered in such a way as to give proper emphasis to the *gist* of the question—here the focus is on Select Committees (you are being asked about the Civil Service and Parliament as an explanation for the weak position of Select Committees, and consequently this should be reflected in your answer).

Slightly different issues arise in relation to the 'critically evaluate' type of question. Such questions usually ask you to assess the success or appropriateness of a particular institution or area of law, as well as to explain what it is. Essentially, they can be divided into two sub-categories:

A Evaluation in a vacuum

In this case you must decide for yourself what criteria of assessment should be used. You should ask yourself what is the institution or law? What can or should it be expected to achieve? And, finally, which standards are you using to justify your choice? Remember that there may be multiple or even competing objectives. If this is the case, then this should be acknowledged and incorporated into your answer—indeed, this may be a reason why the institution or the law in question is not successful.

Examples of such questions are:

> Critically evaluate the constitutional position of political parties in the United Kingdom.

Or:

> Are the existing rules governing the composition of the House of Lords justifiable?

B Evaluation against standards supplied in the question

Here the bulk of the discussion must take place in the light of the particular criteria identified in the question, but the good student may wish to point out that these are not the only, or most important, standards against which the law or institution should be measured. The question itself may ask you, implicitly or explicitly, to assess the importance of the given criteria, through the use of words such as 'sufficient' or 'adequate'.

Examples are:

> To what extent are the rules and principles of judicial review capable of providing clear guidance to public officials as to the boundaries of lawful administrative action?

Or:

> Does English law give sufficient protection to people's right to protest?

A variation on these two categories of question might be to ask you to suggest appropriate reforms. In such reform type questions—say: 'Is the law on homicide in need of reform?'—it is not uncommon to get only 'half the story'. It would, for example, be wrong, or at least foolhardy, to spend all of your time when answering such a question to discuss various reform options if you had not first spent at least *some* of your answer outlining the law on homicide and identifying its alleged weaknesses. It is your assessment of the weaknesses in the current law which would dictate what reforms, if any, you felt were needed. This may seem pretty obvious, but it is quite remarkable how casually students interpret most questions, especially when operating under exam conditions.

Of course, many essay questions afford able students a certain degree of latitude to manipulate their material and thus emphasize certain aspects of the law with which they are more familiar. However, this is a far cry from saying that students are given *carte blanche* to write about whatever they want. Rather, the point is that with an essay question there is, legitimately, a *wider spectrum of possible answers* than with, say, a problem question. That said, the candidate must still interpret the question and supply material which is 'within the ballpark' of most people's understanding of what is really being asked by the examiner. Consequently, if the question being asked is:

> The concept of just deserts defines the boundaries of the extent of permissible punishment in any individual case. Deviation from this norm should not be permitted on utilitarian grounds.
> **Do you agree?**

Then, whatever way you decided to answer this question (agreeing with the quotation or disagreeing with it), the following issues would need to be addressed:

- What is the 'just deserts' theory?
- What problems exist with the just deserts theory?
- What do utilitarian grounds mean?
- Can one justify deviation from the just deserts theory on utilitarian grounds?

Or, if the question was:

> In the light of your understanding of the relationship (or otherwise) between law and morality, explain how you would have decided the appeal to the House of Lords in *Brown* (the sado-masochism case).

Then, whatever way you decide to answer this question (pro-*Brown* or anti-*Brown*), the following issues would have to be addressed:

- What were the issues raised by the *Brown* decision?
- What is the link between law and morality? (Hart/Devlin debate)
- In what way would that debate influence your decision in *Brown*?

Although you may legitimately decide to give some of these issues more weight than others, they all still need to be addressed somewhere in your answer.

Problems of interpretation are particularly apt to arise where students prepare answers in advance of an exam—which to some extent is a necessary part of exam preparation (see later at pp 115–116). However, all too often the pre-prepared material is presented in the exam in a way which is poorly 'tailored' to meet the needs of the particular question posed. This reveals an inability by the student to adapt to a new situation or question, and typifies an inflexibility of mind when faced with a new challenge. By failing to engage in the process of selection and tailoring, the student amply demonstrates that s/he is incapable of performing one of the key tasks which the exam is designed to gauge: whether the candidate can, in relation to the specific question set, distinguish between relevant and irrelevant information. As we have already seen in relation to writing problem answers, success in essay writing is, in many senses, as much to do with what you leave out as it is with what you include. In short, it is about being able to discriminate in relation to the material you have been set to master.

Admittedly, working out exactly what it is that the question is driving at is not always straightforward. Usually the material with which you will have to grapple is complex and, as a result, it can sometimes be easy to misunderstand or misinterpret the question—or, even, be unaware of some hidden danger contained in it. Since 'tricky' questions are, in effect, an occupational hazard for students, either you will need to learn to spot such questions and then leave them well alone; or you will need to face up to the reality of having to read more about your subject. The fact is, the more familiar you are with the secondary literature—books, articles, case-notes, and so on—the more equipped you will be to identify what issue(s) the question is specifically addressing, as well as the range of possible answers that are likely to be found acceptable by the examiner.

Surprisingly, too few students seem to appreciate the need for more than a passing familiarity with the secondary literature. Although initially you will no doubt wish to filter your interpretation of the question through the lens of your lecture notes and any notes you have made from textbooks, this will rarely be enough. Contrary to what you might think (or have been told by students who are supposedly more 'advanced' in their studies), the law journal articles that you are asked to read do not represent the 'icing on the cake'—at least for exam purposes or assessments; instead they represent the 'meat and drink' of your essay answers, helping you to put the question in context, and providing you with arguments for and against various propositions, as well as offering views on how legal disputes could or should be resolved, and presenting the rationales for different legal rules. In short, if you have failed to read the relevant secondary literature, you will struggle to write a good essay simply because your knowledge is limited.

Moreover, part of the test which the examiner has set is to see whether you have a good grasp of the academic literature in the particular area to which the question relates. If this literature is relevant to the question you have chosen to answer, it is important that you draw upon it, all the while offering comment and, where necessary, criticism. Failure to refer to any relevant secondary material will be noted by the examiner and you will be marked down accordingly. Although the relevant literature will often be contained in your reading lists, do not be afraid to draw on other sources, such as may be found in the footnotes of your recommended textbook or in the latest law review articles. Examiners are specifically on the lookout for students who have gone beyond the set reading, since this shows an admirable willingness to 'read around' the subject, for which credit will be given.

By the same token, where the question you have chosen to answer revolves around discussion of, say, an appellate decision—e.g. *Hong Kong Fir*, *Williams v Roffey*, or *Woollin*—you will find it difficult to say anything of note unless you have actually read these (and other related) cases in full (rather than merely relying upon second hand knowledge). Indicate to the examiner that you have read the judgments by writing about what was said and by whom. In cases where there has been judicial dissent, you could profitably use the minority's arguments to criticize the majority's viewpoint. Sadly, very few students are capable of displaying in their answers that they have actually read the case (whichever decision it may be) in full. And even where secondary sources (book, articles, case-notes, etc.) are offered, it is extremely rare for these to extend beyond the usual standard works. The fact is, the more widely read you are, the better able you will be to identify the underlying meaning of any particular essay question and the more capable you will be of marshalling relevant material in response to it. Answers which draw on a range of secondary sources, or which indicate that you have read the case(s) in full, stand out from the pack by a proverbial mile and make an examiner much more inclined to award high marks.

It is also worth pointing out that familiarity with more than what is in your lecture notes or basic textbook will give your work real depth, and thus help solve another recurring problem with many exam answers: more often than not, the answers provided by students are simply too short and lacking in sufficient detail. Instead they tend to 'gloss over' important points and often fail to 'unpack' even basic ideas and concepts. Although a shortish answer may be entirely acceptable provided the material is well directed and elegantly expressed, such answers are in fact very rare indeed. Often times, first-class answers are *at least* 3–4 sides long, and experience indicates that many students are simply unaware of, rather than being unable to produce, the *level of detail* required to score a really good mark. Yet irrespective of the merits of a long answer over a short answer, reading around the subject is likely to provide you with more pertinent things to say in relation to the question which you have chosen to answer.

2 Structuring your answer and devising an argument

Having decided what the question is driving at, and having identified the material which you will need to tackle the question, the next thing you must do is order your thoughts. Indeed, since the meaning of most questions is reasonably clear and the materials with which the majority of students are familiar is roughly similar, the main distinguishing feature between answers is often *structural*. A well-structured answer which addresses *some* of the main points will generally be awarded more marks than a poorly structured answer which covers *most* of the main points. A well-structured answer is evidence of a well-ordered mind, and a well-ordered mind is something which the examiner is keen to see and for which credit will be given.

Sometimes—indeed, often—it will be possible to take your structure from the question;

other times, however, you will need to devise your own structure. Consequently, how you go about structuring your answer will depend very much on the question that has been set.

A Answers which need only be descriptive

Where the question is an 'Explain' or 'Describe' type question, then, generally speaking, all you need to do is present your material within a good, clear, tight framework, and support it with relevant authority. In other words, there is no need to advance an argument. Instead, the key challenge—assuming you know what the question is driving at and have something to say about it—is whether you can stamp some organizing framework over a mass of seemingly disparate material, all the while making it digestible to the reader.

Some of the ways in which material can be marshalled for these purposes have already been touched upon in earlier chapters of this book, but there is no harm in underscoring some of them here. As was mentioned earlier, the most popular method is to outline the general rule that applies and then to list the different exceptions to this rule. For example:

Question

In what circumstances is there criminal liability for omissions in English law?

There can be no mistaking what this question is driving at, and a straightforward exposition, or description, of the relevant law will suffice.

Suggested answer

There is no general principle of liability in English criminal law for failing to act. Thus, the governing rule is that no liability will attach to A if she watches B drown in a shallow pond, even if rescue by A would have been easy. However, in a number of instances a failure to act can constitute the *actus reus* of a criminal offence:

(a) where the definition of the offence actually specifies an omission to act (e.g. failing to file an income tax form when required to do so);

(b) where a special relationship exists between the parties (e.g. parent/child relationship);

(c) where a duty has been voluntarily assumed (e.g. *Stone v Dobinson* (1977); *Instan* (1893));

(d) where a duty arises by way of a contract (e.g. *Pitwood* (1902));

(e) where the defendant creates a dangerous situation (e.g. *Miller* (1983));

(f) where the defendant is under a duty to control others (e.g. *Tuck v Robinson* (1970) where a publican was convicted of aiding and abetting unlawful drinking due to his failure to prevent his customers from so doing).

If, for example, you needed to flesh this out more, one obvious way to do so would be to discuss—by way of illustration—the facts of some of the cases.

Although in the material outlined below, the wording is slightly different, the organizing framework—general rule/exceptions—is the same:

Traditionally, English law has been reluctant to impose liability on people who have failed to act in a particular way, except for identifiable circumstances where they are deemed to be under a specific duty to do so. The circumstances when English law deems a person to be under such a duty are as follows: First . . . **[see the material presented above]**.

Despite the undoubted simplicity of this approach, its utility as a way of organizing your work should not to be discounted.

Of course, it may be that over time the 'exceptions' which the law has developed multiply to such an extent that they are, in fact, so numerous as to 'eat up' the general rule. Should this be the case, a new, more appropriate, restatement of the relevant law will be needed—one that more accurately characterizes the state of the law in that area. Alternatively, it may well be that the area of law is confused and that there exists a great deal of difficulty in mapping out its exact parameters—for example, the law on recovery for pure economic loss. One way to deal with a difficult area like this, is to focus on aspects that are (or are thought to be) clear, and *then* to move on to discuss some of the more debatable areas.

Other techniques include the use of 'principled' objections and 'pragmatic' objections. For example:

Question

All contracts should be of 'utmost good faith', requiring disclosure by the offeror of all material facts.
Discuss.

How about this as an opening sentence (from which the structure of the answer is drawn):

Although there is much that is commendable in a duty of general disclosure **[1]**, there are *principled objections* **[2]** as well as *practical difficulties* **[3]** which make alteration of the law in this area ultimately undesirable.

[1]   Outline why a general duty might be thought to be commendable—e.g. help eradicate the worst aspects of exploitation/offeror may be lowest cost provider of information which is central to the conclusion of a mutually beneficial agreement.

[2]   Outline principled objections:

explain policy behind/rationale for 'strict' rule at common law—a general duty would 'interfere' with this rationale—e.g. introducing unnecessary paternalism/interfering with the 'free' market/force people to give up competitive advantages/where potential injustices remain, can be dealt with by exceptions established at common law or by statute.

[3]   Outline practical objections:

explain difficulty of 'framing' a new general duty—e.g. defining word 'material', could lead to greater uncertainty in business.

[4]   Conclusion.

Despite the superficial attractions of a general duty to contract in good faith, such a development could do more harm than good. Indeed, there is no indication that the existing mix of common law—supplemented, where appropriate, by statutory exceptions—currently leads to glaring injustice.

Alternatively, you could organize your material around the idea that while 'X' may be a necessary condition in demonstrating 'Y', it is not a sufficient one; or on the basis of an orthodox/revisionist split; or even that the rule under discussion is both under-inclusive and over-inclusive—though you would, of course, need to support all these claims with pertinent examples. The point is that, whatever issue you are dealing with, you must seek to stamp some overarching order on it. This is a major part of what an essay question is designed to test.

Sometimes academics and/or judges are able to devise a rationale which explains a specific area of case law, and which can be used to good effect for exam purposes. Take, for example, the doctrine of 'substantial performance' in contract law. In some cases there is said to have been substantial performance of the contract (see *Hoenig v Issacs* [1952] 2 All ER 176), whereas in others there is said not to be (see *Bolton v Mahadeva* [1972] 1 WLR 1009). The art of good textbook writing is to be able to synthesize apparently disparate/inconsistent decisions such as these. Beatson attempts such a synthesis by suggesting that, where the defective performance is a significant proportion of the overall contract price (as in *Bolton* where the cost of remedying the defect was 31 per cent of the contract price), the doctrine of substantial performance does not operate. But where the defect is only a minor proportion of the contract price (as in *Hoenig*, where the cost of remedying the defect was only 7.3 per cent of the contract price), the doctrine of substantial performance does apply.[2] This particular characterization is not necessarily something that the judges sat down and decided before they gave judgment in the above cases. Instead, it is something which has been drawn out of the decisions by Beatson who has sought to take an aerial view of the material in order to make sense of it.

Another example of drawing out 'organizing principles' from apparently disparate case law relates to mistake in criminal law. Cases such as *Morgan* [1976] AC 182, HL, *Williams (Gladstone)* (1984) 78 Cr App R 276, CA, *Beckford* [1988] AC 130, PC, and *Kimber* (1984) 77 Cr App R 225, CA, all support the proposition that the law will accept an honest, albeit unreasonable, mistake in relation to the availability of a defence (a subjective approach); whereas *Fotheringham* (1989) 88 Cr App R 207, CA, *O'Grady* [1987] QB 995, and *Graham* [1982] 1 WLR 294, would seem to support a more limited reading of the law on mistake—and that perhaps in these circumstances only a reasonable mistake has legal relevance (an objective test). How can these two strands of case law be reconciled? One plausible explanation is that where the mistake relates to a justificatory defence (e.g. self-defence, consent, and so on) the subjective view will suffice, but where the mistake relates to an excusatory defence (e.g. drunkenness, duress, and so on) it must be reasonable.[3] Again, this distinction is not something that the judges have necessarily given any thought to before they gave judgment in the above cases. Instead, it is an observation that has been made by someone who is seeking to bring order to an

---

2. Beatson, *Anson's Law of Contract* (28th edn, 2002, Oxford, OUP) 512 n 118.
3. See, Clarkson & Keating, *Criminal Law: Text and Materials* (5th edn, 2003, London, Sweet & Maxwell), 200–1 (where this observation is made, although not necessarily endorsed).

apparently irreconcilable body of case law. Indeed, we could even go so far as to suggest that if a new case were to arise, we *could* employ this justificatory/excusatory distinction as a means of determining the way in which the case would (and perhaps should) be decided, and where it would (and perhaps should) fit into the legal framework. There is nothing fixed or rigid about the above classification—indeed, in Anglo-American jurisprudence the distinction between justifications and excuses is ill-developed—but it does provide a useful framework within which to marshall the relevant authorities.

Note that cases which do not fit into an established classification are often described as 'anomalies'.

B Answers where an argument is required

It has been said that the key to writing a good essay answer is 'to pile up an argument, sentence by sentence to produce a powerful mixture of facts and opinions which wins the day'.[4] In this respect, most examiners seem to favour 'bold, aggressive and original essay writing' rather than an approach which is 'cautious [or] discursive' in style.[5] Indeed, in the words of one examiner, an answer should have 'the punch of a *Sun* editorial and the persuasive concision of one of Alistair Cooke's "Letters from America" '.[6] Likewise, according to the famous playwright Alan Bennett, getting a first at Oxford was not so much about being well read, or even being well educated; rather it was about 'approaching exams journalistically'. In his opinion, the best answers bore a 'striking resemblance to a *Times* leader'.[7]

However, to the extent that students actually proffer views in exam answers, these tend to be much less forthright. This is not surprising—it takes a lot of confidence to express an opinion on an issue which leading legal academics have discussed for years and about which they have failed to come up with a definitive solution. However, while it may sometimes pay to be cautious, your examiner will sense if you are too deferential to the material under consideration and is likely to mark you down accordingly.

A common approach which students adopt is to put the question asked in context, recognizing that there are arguments going both ways. They will then proceed to outline those arguments and, in their conclusion (it is hoped), come down on one side or the other by doing one of two things. Either they will lurch off by writing something along the lines of:

- 'In my opinion . . .', or 'I think . . .', or 'I believe . . .'

Or:

- 'In the light of the above-mentioned criticisms, it seems that . . .' (and their view(s) follow on from this).

---

4. *Independent on Sunday*, 22 May 1994.
5. *The Guardian*, 12 July 1994.
6. Philip Thody, 'Top Marks for Restraint', *Times Higher Educational Supplement*, 15 July 1991.
7. *The Guardian*, 22 May 2004.

This whole approach is a very conventional way of tackling an essay question and, it must be said, if done properly (i.e. if the conclusion really does follow on from the material which preceeds it), will score reasonable marks. However, it is also a very pedestrian approach and tends to be unrewarding for an examiner to mark. It is, despite the begrudging decision to jump one way or the other, an exercise in fence-sitting—the favourite pastime of many exam candidates. The student is simply too tentative, too afraid to commit him/herself to a particular point of view until the very last moment for fear of appearing biased or blinkered. Yet, by adopting this type of approach, students give the impression that their views are tagged on at the end of the essay and are not a fully integrated part of the answer (which is so often the case).

Although a partisan answer is a poor answer, generally speaking in order to score first-class marks in an essay question (admittedly very much depends on the particular question), your answer will need to have a 'thesis'—that is, some point of view, or claim, which will put your work on the 'legal map' in relation to the question posed (see Part C, Q 1 [Option 1] below, at pp 112–113—what thesis do you think is offered in the outline answer?). The examiner will then be able to identify where you stand vis-à-vis other writers on the subject, and your answer will not seem like an endless trawl through all the academics who have ever written on the subject. In other words, you need to develop **your own line of argument**, albeit that you recognize that other writers disagree with you and that there are credible alternative approaches (much like academics do when they write articles in the 'top' law journals). In other words, although you need to take into account the fact that there are arguments going in the other direction, you nevertheless need to show how these arguments can be countered or minimized in view of other factors. In this way, you will have committed yourself to a particular position; you will have developed your own argument as to why you have done so; and your answer will be balanced in the sense that you will have recognized opposing arguments, but shown them to be unpersuasive. Your claims can, of course, be rather modest (e.g. variations on: 'reform in haste, repent at leisure', 'if it ain't broke, don't fix it' and so on); and, *it is stressed again that very much will depend on the wording of the question.*

Of course, the problem with the above suggested strategy is not just that such an answer is difficult to construct, but that it is risky. *You run the risk of devising claims that cannot credibly be supported by the evidence which you have marshalled.* However, when a student successfully manages to engage with the question set in the ways suggested above, examiners uniformly find such answers more rewarding to read and are, therefore, very much more inclined to award them high marks.

As you can see from the material below, such answers do not need to be wonderfully original, or incredibly accomplished, but need merely to be professional in the sense that the material presented and the arguments outlined are both competently and confidently expressed. Examiners want to know what you think and why. More specifically, the examiner wants to know your argument—since it is the quality of your written submission which the examiner marks, irrespective of whether you personally hold the argument that you present. After all, lawyers often argue points of view in court (quite convincingly) to which they are not necessarily committed.

Despite the fact that, as with problem answers, there is no one method by which to write a good essay answer, there are, nonetheless, recognized techniques which can be used to produce a polished answer. These are set out below and are illustrated by way of accompanying examples drawn from law journal articles, judgments, and student answers:

(a) In addition to knowing where your essay is going to end up (i.e. which way you will jump), it is often a good idea to explain clearly the steps which you will take in order to get there. In other words, your answer is like a path that needs signposts to help the reader negotiate the material. For example, you should make clear different 'families' of arguments:

> There are four arguments which support this view. First, ... Secondly, ... Thirdly, ... Lastly, ...
> **[Or, instead of 'lastly': 'The final argument that can be levelled against ... is ...': this reminds the reader which set of arguments you are discussing.]**

In a longer piece of work, e.g. a dissertation or a long essay, it may prove useful to break the material up using headings, and perhaps briefly outline in your introduction what each section will cover. A quick glance at many of the longer articles in any of the good law journals is, usually, illustrative of this point.

(b) In helping to marshall your arguments, make use of what might be called 'turning words' (i.e. words which indicate that the 'flow' of your argument is about to change direction). For example: however, but, yet, nevertheless, nonetheless, notwithstanding, despite this, by contrast, and so on. The same goes for 'reinforcing words', which are used to link up arguments that belong to the same 'family'. Examples include: furthermore, likewise, similarly, moreover, etc. Again, the use of such words should be clear from a quick glance at any well-written law journal article. However, note that you must not overplay your hand in this respect, and since these words stand out, they must be used in the correct context. For example, there is no point in using a 'By contrast' if the material that follows does not support the contrast you are seeking to make; or if the 'moreover' does not help drive home the point you are trying to make.

(c) It may be useful at times to employ arguments that go against your thesis, but which you specifically mention with the aim of 'shooting them down'. Remember, however, that your argument will be weakened if you misrepresent an argument which goes against the case you are trying to make. It is probably best to do justice to competing arguments and then to go on to show how they are fallacious or unsatisfactory in some significant respect.

(d) Outline the general principle or abstract position first and then follow up with a concrete example.

(e) Your answer should demonstrate your ability to make fine distinctions. You may, for example, agree with the outcome of a decision, but deplore the reasoning used to justify it (because although the outcome may be 'just' on the facts of the case, the reasoning may be too broad and thus lead to an unwarranted extension of the rule when applied in a future case). A classic example is *Caldwell* [1982] AC 341 (discussed in Chapter 1)—many would agree that the defendant was culpable and thus deserving of punishment, but equally the basis of the decision was widely regarded as being too broad (in that it failed to take into account whether the defendant *had the capacity to appreciate* the risk he had created). Not surprisingly, the decision has since been overruled by the House of Lords (see *R v G and R* [2003] 3 WLR 1060).

(f) As with cases, do not be led by the academic authorities. Rather, impose your own structure on the material you have been asked to consider. You need to use the academic authorities—much as you use cases—as examples of different ways of viewing the problem under discussion. In other words, avoid a long list of different views which academics hold: 'Atiyah thinks that . . . Treitel believes . . . Collins argues . . . [and so on]'.

(g) Familiarize yourself with appropriate 'lawyerly' language. For example: 'this interpretation would emasculate the Act'; 'there exists a lacuna in the legislation'; 'a question arises whether the common law is abrogated'; 'this is yet another decision which signals a judicial retreat from . . .'; 'there is some support for this proposition from the case law'; 'this line of reasoning was seized upon in the more recent first instance decision of . . .'; 'a more charitable interpretation was taken by the Court of Appeal in . . .'; 'this represents a revisionist view of the case law on . . .'; 'the orthodox approach regarding . . .'; 'the decision in X represents a retrograde step'; 'Treitel has expressed reservations about this view', and so on.

By the same token, avoid incomplete expressions like 'A will be liable'. Liable for what?

(h) Equally, take care with your use of legal terminology and language. In relation to the former avoid sloppy errors such as: recission; estoppel; obitur; unequitable; and so on. Regarding the latter, avoid tautologous expressions such as: 'clear and unambiguous'; 'complete panacea'; 'very unique'; 'reiterated again'; 'merging together', and so on. The point is that good essays must be finely crafted, and must show good attention to detail as well as an appreciation of nuance and tone.

(i) One last point. Some law examiners prefer you to express your views in terms of impartial submissions (e.g. 'therefore it is submitted that . . .') rather than 'I think . . .'. Other examiners, however, prefer you to be more direct; your answer is, after all, personal and subjective, and to try to cover it with a veil of false objectivity is disingenuous. Nonetheless, nearly all examiners will be appalled by 'In my opinion', 'I feel that . . .', or worse, 'I personally think . . .'; or 'I believe . . .'. Instead, try: 'In this essay I will argue that . . .'; or, in summing up, 'I have argued that . . .'; or 'My argument is . . .'. Whatever approach you adopt, do not overplay it, or let it become intrusive.

To summarize, in order to turn out a good answer you need to make effective use of the above-mentioned techniques. Your models in this respect should be the books, articles, case-notes, and judgments you are asked to read. Some such 'models' are set out below.

Simon Gardner's, 'Duress in Attempted Murder' (1991) 107 LQR 389:

> The Court of Appeal has decided that duress is no defence to attempted murder: *R v Gotts* [1991] 2 WLR 878. In *R v Howe* [1987] AC 417 the House of Lords had decided that duress was no defence to murder itself, [hence] the extension of this rule to [attempted murder] might have been thought predictable. However, an examination of the decision [in *Gotts*] raises questions about its sustainability—and, in turn, that of *Howe* . . .

There, in the space of a few lines, Gardner summarizes the law and, more importantly for the purposes of illustration here, sets out his stall by telling us exactly what he hopes the case-note will achieve. We are left in no doubt as to where Gardner stands: he likes neither *Gotts* nor *Howe* and he is determined to share with us his reasons for this antipathy. In the remainder of the material Gardner seeks to justify this point of view. His short note has all the hallmarks of the sort of approach which you could usefully emulate.

Gardner's short case-note also demonstrates other helpful points. For example:

> **[A]** Late in 1990, terrorists persuaded members of the public, by holding hostage their families, to drive vehicles loaded with explosives into military checkpoints.... According to *Howe* these drivers were guilty of murder. It appears that, on the contrary, they are not being charged with any offence. The practical disposal of the case again reveals dissatisfaction with the principle of *Howe*. **[B]** It might be rejoined here ... that *Howe* should be read as allowing for the non-prosecution of meritorious cases of murder under duress ... their Lordships in *Howe* took this very point.... **[C]** But ... only the clutched straw of unreviewable executive discretion prevents this from being a flat contradiction of the fundamental proposition [outlined in *Howe*] that for moral or instrumental reasons murder under duress cannot be pardoned.

In this passage:

[A] Gardner criticizes the rationale in *Howe*.

[B] He then sets up a counter argument: 'It might be rejoined . . .'

[C] He hits this counter argument 'for six', reinforcing his favoured position.

Consider, also, the following passage from Janet O'Sullivan's case-note, 'Remoteness of Damage in Negligence: A Rotten Structure Collapses' [1999] CLJ 12:

> In *The Wagon Mound (No 1)* [1961] AC 388, Viscount Simmonds expressed the hope that, by replacing directness ... with reasonable foreseeability as the test for remoteness of damage in negligence, 'the law will be simplified and ... palpable injustice will be avoided.' Lawyers have long recognised that the first of these aspirations has failed dismally. Regrettably, the Court of Appeal decision in *Jolley v Sutton London Borough Council* [1998] 1 WLR 1546 provides a stark example of failure on both counts.

If the question were 'Assess the decision in *Jolley v Sutton*', this would be as good an introduction as any. It puts the decision in context and, again, leaves the reader in no doubt about where the author stands regarding the case and the issues which it raises.

However, you do not need to be so forthright at the beginning of your answer, as the following piece, by Burrows, on the controversial doctrine of consideration in English law, illustrates:[8]

> The requirements of consideration—that something requested must be given in return for a promise in order to make it binding—ensures that only bargain promises, and not gratuitous promises, are enforceable in English law. In civil law systems this is not so and, even in England, there are a number of exceptions to the need for consideration, which cast doubt on its

8. A. Burrows, *Understanding the Law of Obligations: Essays on Contract, Tort and Restitution* (2000, Oxford, Hart Publishing), reproduced with kind permission of Hart Publishing.

underlying validity. In particular, a promise contained in a deed is valid, whether or not there is consideration; proprietary estoppel protects a promisee's expectations of being given proprietary rights where the promisee has detrimentally relied on a promise to be given such rights; and promissory estoppel may operate to prevent a promisor breaking a promise to give up existing rights where the promisee has relied on that promise. There are also very specific exceptions, for example documentary letters of credit and compositions with creditors.

The decision of the Court of Appeal in *Williams v Roffey Bros & Nicholls (Contractors) Ltd* raises further difficulties. In that case it was held that a head-contractor's promise to pay sub-contracting joiners extra money to complete their pre-existing contractual duties on time was a binding promise, supported by consideration, albeit that the promise would have been voidable if made under economic duress. The consideration was deemed to be the 'practical benefit' of the work being completed on time even though the head-contractor was already contractually entitled to that and, in one sense therefore, did not receive anything extra or different in return for its promise.

If one accepts that performance of, or a promise to perform, a pre-existing duty is good consideration for a promise to pay extra, it is hard to see why, applying the same logic, part performance, or a promise to perform part, of a pre-existing duty should not be good consideration for a promise to give up an entitlement to full performance. While one must again be careful not to enforce promises entered into under duress, it would seem that in line with *Williams v Roffey* there is a 'practical benefit' to promisors in receiving part performance, where the practical alternative may be no performance at all. Yet three Court of Appeal cases since *Williams v Roffey* [—*Re Selectmove* (1995); *R C a Debtor* (1994); and *Ferguson v Davies* (1997)—] have adhered to the traditional view, established in *Foakes v Beer*, that such promises are not supported by consideration and are therefore unenforceable. The cases have also either marginalized, or ignored, the potential operation on these facts of promissory estoppel.

The picture is therefore one of incoherence and some uncertainty. It represents English law struggling to decide whether to enforce informal gratuitous promises and deciding that, in some circumstances but not all, it should do so. The law would be rendered more intelligible and clear if the need for consideration were abolished and gratuitous promises that have been accepted or relied on were held to be binding (subject to the operation of normal contractual rules relating to, for example, the intention to create legal relations, duress, and illegality).

Note, how the material . . . but the material is handled with an assurance and elegance which belies its simplicity. Unlike earlier with Gardner's case-note, and the piece by O'Sullivan, here the 'sting' is in the tail. Burrows waits until his conclusion before he reveals his hand, albeit that the main body of the work is written with his trenchant criticism in mind.

The rest of this chapter is devoted to applying some of the above-mentioned techniques to (a) an exam question on the criminal law of omissions; and (b) an exam question relating to the law on consideration.

C Criminal law

Question

English criminal law should either introduce a general duty to act to save imperilled persons, or, alternatively, expand the present list of situations when one is under a duty to act.
Discuss.

Relevant ideas

The material set out below represents some of the ideas that would need to be covered in order to provide a respectable answer to the question posed. As we shall see, this material is used to fashion two contrasting answers in terms of both argument and structure.

One of the suggestions which has been made in this area is the introduction of a duty of 'easy rescue' (Ashworth, 'The Scope of Criminal Liability for Omissions' (1989) 105 LQR 424).

There are sound arguments in favour of a duty of easy rescue:

A duty of easy rescue

- it is immoral not to render assistance when it is well within one's powers to do so; criminal law should be a reflection of a moral world;
- attention should be focused on punishing conduct which causes a particular harm irrespective of whether the harm results from an act of commission or and 'act' of omission;
- arguments that a general duty to act would be contrary to individual liberty and autonomy ignore the value that individuals place on interpersonal support and relationships;
- the law is justified in using coercion to force people to take actions required to improve the options and opportunities of others;
- the reduction in the autonomy of an individual will be offset as the level of autonomy in the community as a whole rises.

At the same time there are a number of forceful objections, both in principle and in practice, to this line of argument:

Objections in principle

- criminal liability is premised on our concepts of *mens rea* and *actus reus*, which denote control—these are relevant to the defendant's positive actions rather than his failure to counter a risk not caused by him;
- it will inhibit people's personal autonomy;
- the difficulty of establishing the requisite causal link between the defendant's inactivity and the harms that occur (a person cannot 'cause' a result by doing nothing);
- values such as charity or courage will be eroded because people will have no real choice but to act in accordance with the law;
- there is something morally repugnant about holding an individual responsible for an independent process over which he or she exerts no control;
- 'luck' would be allowed to play an unwarranted part in the criminal law, e.g. the unlucky bystander who is under an obligation to rescue;

- the wealthy person who fails to give to the starving beggar would be liable for a criminal offence—such a law could undermine the capitalist work ethic;

- since a general duty can be defined only in broad terms, prosecutors would have too much discretion—this breaches the principle of maximum certainty (liability should be well-defined).

Pragmatic objections

- the jury in the safety of court might have a different view of what is 'easy rescue';
- an incompetent rescuer could cause more harm than good;
- who would be the rescuer in a crowd of people?

The above ideas can now be used to fashion two distinct answers, each positing a different line of argument—Answer A (arguing for the status quo), and Answer B (critical of the status quo and arguing for law reform).

Suggested answer A

In 'The Scope of Criminal Liability for Omissions', Ashworth argues for a duty of 'easy rescue' where no unreasonable risk, cost, or inconvenience would be incurred by the potential rescuer. Yet despite the superficial attractions of such an approach, fundamental problems are caused by the expansion of criminal liability that a new general duty of easy rescue would inevitably entail. In any case, as I seek to show, the existing categories of criminal liability are adequate.

The case for a general duty to act to save imperilled persons rests on the view that it is clearly immoral not to render assistance when it is well within one's powers to do so. The criminal law should be a reflection of a moral world. Accordingly, attention should be focused on punishing conduct which causes a particular harm irrespective of whether the harm is a result of commission or omission. Arguments that such a general duty to act would be contrary to individual liberty and autonomy ignore the value that individuals place on interpersonal support and relationships. As Raz argues, the law is justified in using coercion to force people to take actions required to improve the options and opportunities of others. The reduction in the autonomy of an individual is offset to the extent that the level of autonomy in the community as a whole increases.

While forceful, these arguments are by no means compelling. As Meade (1991) claims, coercing an individual to give attention to others in itself represents a threat to his own autonomy. If society is prepared to sacrifice an individual's autonomy in order to save a life, how many other rights of individuals will be ignored for some—supposedly justifiable—greater good? Furthermore, forcing people to act through fear of legal sanction would involve the erosion of important values such as courage or charity . . .

[You could then discuss the adequacy of existing categories of liability; see above at pp 101–102.]

Suggested answer B

The question asks us to consider alternative ways of improving the criminal law of omissions. In order to answer this it is first necessary to explain why it might be thought that the existing law is inadequate. I will then go on to consider the suitability of the different reform options which have been mooted.

Weaknesses in the existing law

[Here you would discuss the existing law and any weaknesses in it e.g. a bystander who watches a small child die when rescue was easy is not liable.]

Moral justification for extension

[Here you could outline the arguments to support an extension of the existing duty.]

Limitations of duty

[Here you could outline arguments to limit this duty based on practical problems; your ultimate argument could be that the defendant should not be liable for the 'full' offence, but for a specific offence of 'failure to act'.]

Conclusion

[Here you could say that a 'failure to act' approach satisfies the moral need to punish, while at the same time recognizing fundamental philosophical and practical objections to holding people liable for the full offence.]

As you can see, the same material has been used to produce contrasting answers, potentially of equal worth. Answer A (arguing for a retention of the status quo) gets off to a very strong start. Within the first few sentences, it is clear that the student has understood the issues which need to be addressed by the question, and there is even a hint of the 'gist' of the argument which is to follow. Moreover, the introduction supplies the structure which is to be employed in order to present the material to good effect. Answer B (suggesting that reform is needed and indicating how it may be satisfactorily achieved) is, however, no less impressive. This is so, despite the fact that a different approach is adopted, and despite the fact that there is no indication at the beginning of the answer where the writer stands. Whatever the desirability of one conclusion over the other—and this is an issue on which there is no answer in any conclusive sense—both answers reflect a fair degree of sophistication and clarity and, prima facie, merit the award of high marks.

D Contract law

Again, some of the earlier mentioned advice can be seen at work in the material dealt with below, involving *Foakes v Beer*.

Question

Foakes v Beer should be overruled. **Discuss.**

Below we use broadly the same material to set out three 'skeleton answers', all illustrative of many of the techniques so far discussed in this chapter.

Option 1

How about something along these lines as an opening paragraph:

[1] The House of Lords decision in *Foakes v Beer* stands as one of the last bastions of 'classical'

contract law. [2] However, as is shown below, the ruling has already been partially outflanked by the doctrine of promissory estoppel and [3] is out of step with other developments in relation to variation of contracts, such as *William v Roffey*'s 'practical benefit' test. [4] In addition, concerns over creditor protection—which *Foakes v Beer* is said in part to represent—have largely been assuaged by developments in economic duress. [5] The case, therefore, no longer retains the relevance which it formerly did.

[Note how the structure of the answer is drawn from the way in which the material is 'set up' in the introduction (see [1], [2], and so on, below). You do not need to make such bold claims at the beginning of your answer—you could instead 'save' your claims for your conclusion. However, to the extent that you do adopt a less aggressive opening stance, you will nevertheless need to know where you are ultimately going to end up so that you can push your material in that direction.

That is to say, if you do not know where you stand in relation to the question when you begin your answer, it is virtually certain that your conclusion will seem 'detached' from the main body of your work.

In particular, note how the answer takes its structure from the material set out in the opening paragraph]:

[1]   *Foakes v Beer*: an example of classical contract law at its height—explain the case—what was the legal issue raised by the case?—use the key facts to illustrate the principle laid down—outline the significance of the court's decision (in what way is the decision important for people with a similar dispute and does the case have any bearing on contract law more generally?).

However, attacks/developments:

[2]   Denning J in *High Trees* (first attack—but arguably 'reigned in' by subsequent developments in estoppel).

[3]   CA in *Williams v Roffey*—'practical benefit' (second attack—albeit restricted by Peter Gibson LJ in the Court of Appeal case of *Selectmove* [resulting in the creation of an uneasy and probably ultimately unworkable reconciliation where 'payment for goods and services cases' are treated differently from 'debt cases']).

[4]   Developments in economic duress.

[5]   Conclusion—how about:

Foakes v Beer has had its day. Aside from the fact that it has been qualified by way of developments in promissory estoppel, it is out of step with other developments in contract law too. It should either be overruled by the House of Lords (to bring it into line with the more commercially realistic 'practical benefit' test in *Williams v Roffey*) or, after consultation with the Law Commission, legislation should be enacted to outflank its effects.

What is the 'thesis' propounded in this answer? That is to say, what argument, or claim, is being advanced in response to the question? Well, in short, the conclusion pretty much sums it up: the answer is indisputably anti-*Foakes v Beer*. Why? Because the case is, for the reasons mentioned, out of step with modern legal developments. The answer even offers solutions for reform. Despite the fact that the question did not specifically ask for this, it is nevertheless legitimate to include them, in that certain parameters of the question are not fixed.

As we have seen, it is important for the examiner to know where you stand on the central issue(s) raised by the question, and why. Making 'your mark'—placing your ideas on the 'legal map' in relation to the question—is important, since it shows the examiner that you are prepared to adopt a position and defend it. By all means borrow generic arguments from articles and books you have read, but do not overdo this. In other words, do not let a strength (i.e. engaging with the question) become a weakness (by making all sorts of spurious claims that cannot be supported and make you sound as though you are on a 'soap box'). It is not enough merely to assert a particular position. Your claim must be given support, by the use, for example, of legal developments and doctrines—as is the case in the above answer. Doing so helps persuade those who might be inclined to hold an alternative point of view to come round to your way of thinking. Note also that the introduction and the conclusion resonate with one another, giving the whole essay a sense of cohesion. Finally, remember that a good essay is as much to do with tone and nuance (and an appreciation of the two), as it is to do with content.

Option 2

Option 2 represents a more 'arm's length', but no less effective, answer which maintains broadly the same approach as Option 1 above:

> In *Foakes v Beer* **[discuss facts]**. The main issue which the House of Lords had to address was . . . Their Lordships ruled . . . The significance of the case is that . . . **[or discuss the rationale for the ruling. This could take up as much as 2–3 paragraphs].**
>
> While *Foakes v Beer* has stood as a lynch-pin of classical contract law for over a century, recent developments have, however, eroded its central position in contract law and have prompted suggestions for reform. **[Up to this point we have not overtly committed ourselves one way or the other, but have hinted at where the answer is going. And this hint is being introduced a quarter of the way through the answer.]**
>
> First, . . . **[discuss estoppel]**. Secondly, . . . **[discuss developments in consideration generally and *Williams v Roffey* in particular]**. Thirdly, . . . **[discuss economic duress]**.
>
> **[As your conclusion:]** In light of the above developments, *Foakes v Beer* seems oddly out of step with emerging legal trends which challenge the descriptive accuracy of classical contract law. If the common law is to survive, lawyers must learn to let go of cases which have outlived their usefulness—*Foakes v Beer* is one such case.

Although there is no clue given at the beginning of the answer as to where the student stands in relation to the question, the reader is left in no doubt by the time they have finished: as with Option 1, the answer is indisputably anti-*Foakes v Beer*.

Option 3

Option 3 presents an argument—using pretty much the same material—but yet 'going the other way':

The fact that the House of Lords' decision in *Foakes v Beer* has survived for so long, bears testimony both to its durability and its continuing relevance to modern day contract law. As I argue below, overruling *Foakes* at this juncture would amount to a wrong turning point in English law.

[You would then need to explain *Foakes v Beer*—that is, identify the legal issue raised by the decision and use the facts to illustrate the issue, as well as proceed to outline the significance of their Lordships' decision. Following that, you would need to deal with some of the developments which, as it were, 'go against', or undercut, *Foakes v Beer*. Perhaps something along the following lines:]

Admittedly a number of developments can be characterized as having undercut the orthodoxy endorsed in *Foakes* [then discuss: estoppel, *William v Roffey*, economic duress].

[You could then move back to your favoured position, by saying something like:]

However, all of these so-called challenges to *Foakes v Beer* are themselves open to attack ... [Estoppel only protects reliance interests rather than expectation interests; *Williams v Roffey* raises more problems than it solves e.g. the ambiguity of the 'practical benefit' test; and economic duress is an embryonic doctrine which is too uncertain to be relied upon—you would, of course, need to develop these ideas.]

In conclusion, *Foakes v Beer* remains central to the enforeceability of promises and exhibits an element of certainty and simplicity which is sadly lacking in many areas of modern contract law.

3   Practising essay writing

Many students are surprisingly naive when it comes to writing exam essays. Often they assume that quick thinking in the heat of the exam will be sufficient to score high marks. Although this may be true on certain occasions, as a rule a good essay answer will require considered reflection on the issues involved—something which it is extremely difficult to do in the context of an exam where you are under severe time constraints. Consequently, it is particularly important that you try to formulate your ideas and views *before* you enter the exam room rather than while you are in it. This approach requires you to put some time aside—during the year, and certainly at revision time—to *think* about the 'big picture' of how different parts of your course fit together as well as to work out your own 'position' on specific issues. If you take the trouble to do this, you will be in a better position to handle the issues raised by the exam questions you have to face.

Of course, there will be many issues in law school about which you will care little, if at all. It is rare for law students to spend sleepless nights worrying about whether recklessness in the criminal law should be objective or subjective, or where the boundaries should be set for recovery of damages in negligence. Although it almost goes without saying that if you do not care about *any* of the issues which you encounter in law school you might want to reconsider your reasons for being there, the real point to note is that the examiner is not at all interested in the extent to which you care about these matters. Rather, the examiner is interested in your powers of analysis, reasoning, and expression, as reflected in your willingness and ability to *engage with* a question on a (typically complex) legal issue.

It is also a good discipline to experiment with writing answers or outlining arguments which support views that you do not necessarily hold. This will help you to see that there is always at least one other point of view.

Statistically, those students who do not make use of the opportunity to submit written work are at a distinct disadvantage in the exam, since there is always a gap (sometimes a very large one) between what you think you know and what you are actually able to express on paper. Moreover, doing the written work and getting feedback from your tutor, means that you are better aware of what is needed to do well in the exam in terms of style, content, and emphasis. Your revision period is, of course, crucial. Assuming that you do eight hours of revision a day, you should set aside one hour each day (or even every other day) so that you can write an answer to a previous exam question. In this way you are actually practising the skill upon which you will be tested. After you have written the answer, file it away and after a few days return to it with the aim of seeing how it could be improved. There is little about exams that can be guaranteed, but there is a very good chance that anyone who does this will improve their *overall mark in that subject* by as much as 5 per cent. None of this actually involves doing *more* work, rather it merely involves doing *different* work which, in the long run, can be very, very effective. In terms of being successful at the exam game, this is the most important rule of which to be aware and to abide by and, consequently, it is almost certain to be the rule which is most often not followed by students (usually because of the degree of self-discipline involved).

4   Summary

- Above all else you must answer the specific question posed. This, of course, may seem painfully obvious, but it is nevertheless advice which is very often not followed.

- If the question involves a longish quotation, take care over how you interpret it. In particular, avoid taking an overly literal approach. Instead, concentrate on responding to the *gist* of what the question is driving at.

- Reading secondary materials—such as articles and case-notes—is not an optional extra when seeking to score high marks in essay questions. The material in these sources will not only help you to interpret the question and put it into context, but will also provide you with the ammunition you need to answer it.

- In reform-type questions, it would be wrong, or at least foolhardy, to spend all of your time talking about the various reform options if you have not first spent at least *some* of your answer outlining the current law and identifying its alleged weaknesses.

- As with writing answers to problem questions, success in essay writing is, in many senses, as much to do with what you leave out as it is to do with what you include. In short, it is about being able to discriminate in relation to the material you have been set to master.

- A well-structured essay answer which addresses *some* of the main points will generally score more marks than a poorly structured answer which covers *most* of the main points.

- Sometimes—indeed, often—it will be possible to take your structure from the question; other times, however, you will need to devise your own structure.

- Most essay answers must contain a credible thesis—or claim—which you must support with argument rather than assertion.

- Use proper legal jargon.

- Practice makes perfect (or at least it minimizes the risk of things going awry)

3145309R00072

Printed in Great Britain
by Amazon.co.uk, Ltd.,
Marston Gate.